THE HOUSE ON
MANGO STREET

Sandra Cisneros

SPARKNOTES is a registered trademark of SparkNotes LLC

Spark Publishing
A Division of Barnes & Noble
120 Fifth Avenue
New York, NY 10011
www.sparknotes.com

ISBN-13: 978-1-4114-0256-0
ISBN-10: 1-4114-0256-1

Please submit changes or report errors to www.sparknotes.com/errors.

Printed and bound in the United States.

5 7 9 10 8 6 4

Introduction: Stopping to Buy SparkNotes on a Snowy Evening

Whose words these are you *think* you know.
Your paper's due tomorrow, though;
We're glad to see you stopping here
To get some help before you go.

Lost your course? You'll find it here.
Face tests and essays without fear.
Between the words, good grades at stake:
Get great results throughout the year.

Once school bells caused your heart to quake
As teachers circled each mistake.
Use SparkNotes and no longer weep,
Ace every single test you take.

Yes, books are lovely, dark, and deep,
But only what you grasp you keep,
With hours to go before you sleep,
With hours to go before you sleep.

Contents

CONTEXT

S andra Cisneros was born in 1954 in Chicago to a Spanish-speaking Mexican father and an English-speaking mother of Mexican descent. She was the third child and only daughter in a family of seven children. While she spent most of her childhood in one of Chicago's Puerto Rican neighborhoods, she also traveled back and forth to Mexico with her family. Cisneros has published two books of poetry, *My Wicked Wicked Ways* and *Loose Woman*; a children's book titled *Hair/Pelitos*; a collection of stories titled *Woman Hollering Creek and Other Stories*; and, most recently, a second novel, *Caramelo*.

Cisneros is part of a group of Chicana and Latina writers who became prominent in the 1980s and 1990s, among them Gloria Anzaldua, Laura Esquivel, and Julia Alvarez. *Chicana* refers to a woman of Mexican descent who lives in the United States. *Latina* is a more encompassing word, referring to women from all the Latin American countries. These women were part of a larger group of American minority women, such as Amy Tan and Toni Morrison, who found success as writers at the end of the twentieth century. While many of them had been writing for some time, renewed interest in the issues of race and gender in the 1980s provided a milieu in which their work became a vital part of the dialogue taking place.

The House on Mango Street received mostly positive reviews when it was published in 1984, and it has sold more than two million copies worldwide. However, some male Mexican-American critics have attacked the novel, arguing that by writing about a character whose goal is to leave the barrio (a neighborhood or community where most of the residents are of Spanish-speaking origin), Cisneros has betrayed the barrio, which they see as an important part of Mexican tradition. Others have criticized the novel as encouraging assimilation, labeling Cisneros a *vendida*, or sellout. Such critics have condemned Cisneros for perpetuating what they see as negative stereotypes of Mexican-American men (the wife-beaters, the overbearing husbands), while at the same time contending that the feminism Cisneros embraces was created by white women. Cisneros's defenders claim that a Mexican-American woman's experiences are very different from the experiences of a Mexican-American man, and that it's therefore unfair to expect

Cisneros, a woman, to present a unified front with male Mexican-American writers. In *The House on Mango Street*, Cisneros focuses on the problems of being a woman in a largely patriarchal Hispanic society.

The House on Mango Street consists of what Cisneros calls "lazy poems," vignettes that are not quite poems and not quite full stories. The vignettes are sometimes only two or three paragraphs long, and they often contain internal rhymes, as a poem might. This form also reflects a young girl's short attention span, flitting from one topic to another, never placing too much importance on any one event. Within these very short pieces, Cisneros introduces dozens of characters, some only once or twice, and in this way, the structure of the novel imitates the geography of the barrio. No one person has very much space, either in the barrio or on the page, and the neighborhood is small enough that even a young girl can know everyone in it by name. The conflicts and problems in these little stories are never fully resolved, just as the fates of men, women, and children in the barrio are often uncertain. Finally, the novel's structure suggests the variable fate of Chicana women, whose life stories often depend on men. Without a dominant, omniscient, masculine voice to tell the women's stories, their narratives are left waiting and unresolved.

Critics have compared *The House on Mango Street* to Virginia Woolf's *A Room of One's Own*, a long essay in which Woolf asserts that women need a place and financial resources of their own in order to write successfully. The protagonist in *The House on Mango Street*, Esperanza, does long for a place of her own, but writing is a way for her to get that place, not the other way around. In this way, *The House on Mango Street* is more similar to *A House for Mr. Biswas*, by British colonial novelist V. S. Naipaul, in which an Indian in Trinidad struggles to balance his interactions with his wife's extended family and his dream of possessing his own private space. In many ways, *The House on Mango Street* is a traditional bildungsroman—that is, a coming-of-age story. Only one year passes over the course of the novel, but Esperanza matures tremendously during this period. The novel resembles other artists' coming-of-age stories, including James Joyce's *A Portrait of the Artist as a Young Man*. Like the hero of that novel, Stephen Dedalus, Esperanza has a keen eye for observation and is gifted in her use of language.

Though Esperanza experiences two sexual assaults, this work should not be considered a sexual-abuse novel. For the young girls in *The House on Mango Street*, assault is only one aspect, and not a particularly shocking one, of growing up. The assault may change Esperanza's view of sex and men, but it does not make her want to leave the barrio—that desire begins to grow well before the assaults happen. Some feminist critics blame Cisneros for not criticizing men more strongly in the novel. After Esperanza is raped, she does not blame the boys who did it, only the girl who was not there when Esperanza needed her and the women who have not debunked romantic myths about sex. In Esperanza's world, male violence is so ordinary that blaming them for the rape would be unusual. The boys, as she says in an early section, live in their own worlds. By completely separating the men's world from the women's, Cisneros indicts both men and her culture. Her criticism is even more powerful because she veils her anger instead of making it explicit. In *The House on Mango Street*, Cisneros demonstrates her ability to critique her culture without openly or unfairly condemning it.

PLOT OVERVIEW

In a series of vignettes, *The House on Mango Street* covers a year in the life of Esperanza, a Chicana (Mexican-American girl), who is about twelve years old when the novel begins. During the year, she moves with her family into a house on Mango Street. The house is a huge improvement from the family's previous apartment, and it is the first home her parents actually own. However, the house is not what Esperanza has dreamed of, because it is run-down and small. The house is in the center of a crowded Latino neighborhood in Chicago, a city where many of the poor areas are racially segregated. Esperanza does not have any privacy, and she resolves that she will someday leave Mango Street and have a house all her own.

Esperanza matures significantly during the year, both sexually and emotionally. The novel charts her life as she makes friends, grows hips, develops her first crush, endures sexual assault, and begins to write as a way of expressing herself and as a way to escape the neighborhood. The novel also includes the stories of many of Esperanza's neighbors, giving a full picture of the neighborhood and showing the many possible paths Esperanza may follow in the future.

After moving to the house, Esperanza quickly befriends Lucy and Rachel, two Chicana girls who live across the street. Lucy, Rachel, Esperanza, and Esperanza's little sister, Nenny, have many adventures in the small space of their neighborhood. They buy a bike, learn exciting stories about boys from a young woman named Marin, explore a junk shop, and have intimate conversations while playing Double Dutch (jumping rope). The girls are on the brink of puberty and sometimes find themselves sexually vulnerable, such as when they walk around their neighborhood in high-heeled shoes or when Esperanza is kissed by an older man at her first job. During the first half of the year, the girls are content to live and play in their child's world. At school, Esperanza feels ashamed about her family's poverty and her difficult-to-pronounce name. She secretly writes poems that she shares only with older women she trusts.

Over the summer, Esperanza slips into puberty. She suddenly likes it when boys watch her dance, and she enjoys dreaming about them. Esperanza's newfound sexual maturity, combined with the death of two of her family members, her grandfather and her Aunt Lupe, bring her closer to the world of adults. She begins to closely watch the women in her neighborhood. This second half of *The House on Mango Street* presents a string of stories about older women in the neighborhood, all of whom are even more stuck in their situations and, quite literally, in their houses, than Esperanza is. Meanwhile, during the beginning of the following school year, Esperanza befriends Sally, a girl her age who is more sexually mature than Lucy or Rachel. Sally, meanwhile, has her own agenda. She uses boys and men as an escape route from her abusive father. Esperanza is not completely comfortable with Sally's sexual experience, and their friendship results in a crisis when Sally leaves Esperanza alone, and a group of boys sexually assaults Esperanza in her absence.

Esperanza's traumatic experiences as Sally's friend, in conjunction with her detailed observations of the older women in her neighborhood, cement her desire to escape Mango Street and to have her own house. When Esperanza finds herself emotionally ready to leave her neighborhood, however, she discovers that she will never fully be able to leave Mango Street behind, and that after she leaves she'll have to return to help the women she has left. At the end of the year, Esperanza remains on Mango Street, but she has matured extensively. She has a stronger desire to leave and understands that writing will help her put distance between herself and her situation. Though for now writing helps her escape only emotionally, in the future it may help her to escape physically as well.

CHARACTER LIST

MAJOR CHARACTERS

Esperanza The novel's heroine and narrator, an approximately twelve-year-old Chicana (Mexican-American girl). Esperanza is a budding writer who wishes for a home of her own. *The House on Mango Street* chronicles a year in her life as she matures emotionally and sexually. The name Esperanza means "hope" in Spanish.

Rachel and Lucy Esperanza's best friends. Rachel and Lucy are Mexican-American sisters who live across the street from Esperanza. Lucy, the older sister, was born in Texas, while Rachel, the younger, was born in Chicago. Esperanza eventually chooses a more sexually mature friend, Sally.

Sally A young girl Esperanza befriends the same year she moves to Mango Street. Sally is the same age as Esperanza but is sexually bold and seems quite glamorous to Esperanza. She is not a good friend to Esperanza, abandoning her time and again to go off with boys. She has a physically abusive father and runs off before eighth grade to marry a man who won't let her see her friends or leave the house. Esperanza feels protective of Sally.

Nenny Esperanza's little sister. Nenny, whose real name is Magdalena, is a pretty, dreamy little girl for whom Esperanza is often responsible. Since Nenny is immature, she is often a source of embarrassment for Esperanza when the two of them play with Rachel and Lucy.

Marin A young woman from Puerto Rico who lives with her cousin's family. Marin spends most of her time baby-sitting and so cannot leave the house. She sells makeup for Avon and teaches Esperanza and her friends about the world of boys. Although she has a fiancé back in Puerto Rico, she also dreams about American men taking her away from Mango Street to the suburbs. At the end of the year, her cousins send her back to Puerto Rico.

Papa   Esperanza's father. Originally from Mexico, Papa is less domineering than the other father figures in the neighborhood. He works most of the time and is rarely home.

Mama   Esperanza's mother. Mama grew up in the United States. She is one of the strongest-willed and smartest women in the novel, yet she seems to influence Esperanza very little. She is sometimes a source of comfort for Esperanza. All of her admirable attributes are lost on Esperanza because Mama has not escaped Mango Street to live somewhere nicer.

Alicia   Esperanza's friend who attends a local university. Since Alicia's mother died, her father forces her to take over the family's domestic chores. Alicia is a rare example of a neighborhood girl who has not tried to escape the neighborhood through marriage, but instead works hard and hopes to change her life from within.

Cathy   Esperanza's first friend in the neighborhood. Cathy's family moves out the week after Esperanza's family moves in. She discourages Esperanza from becoming friends with Rachel and Lucy. She is one of the few characters who is not from Mexico or Latin America.

Minor characters in order of appearance

Carlos and Kiki Esperanza's younger brothers. Carlos and Kiki appear infrequently, and Esperanza explains that they live in a different, male world.

Meme Ortiz The new resident of Cathy's house. Meme's real name is Juan, and he has a dog with two names.

Louie   The eldest sibling in a Puerto Rican family that lives in the basement of the Ortiz house. Louie is friends with Esperanza's brothers, while Esperanza is friends with Louie's cousin Marin. Louie's other cousin appears once with a stolen car, only to get arrested later that afternoon.

The Vargas Kids An unspecified number of poorly raised, vagrant siblings whose father has abandoned them. One of the Vargas kids, Angel Vargas, dies by falling from a great height.

Uncle Nacho Esperanza's friendly uncle, who gets her to dance at her cousin's baptism in "Chanclas."

Aunt Lupe Esperanza's aunt. In her youth, Lupe was a vibrant, beautiful swimmer, but now she is old, blind, and bed-ridden. She listens to Esperanza's poems and encourages her to keep writing, but Esperanza and her friends mock Lupe behind her back.

Elenita   A witch woman Esperanza visits to have her fortune told. Elenita reads Tarot cards and tells Esperanza that she will have "a home in the heart."

Ruthie   A childish grown-up neighbor who enjoys playing with Esperanza and her friends. Ruthie's mother, Edna, is a landlady for the large building next door and ignores Ruthie.

Geraldo   A Mexican man Marin meets at a dance. Geraldo dies in a car accident the evening she meets him. Nobody, including Marin, knows anything about him, including his last name.

Mamacita The overweight Mexican wife of another neighbor. Mamacita comes to America at great expense to her husband, but she is wildly unhappy. She never learns English and never leaves her third-floor apartment.

Rafaela A neighborhood woman whose husband locks her in their apartment because he is afraid she'll run off. Rafaela sends money down on a clothesline to Esperanza and her friends so they can buy her sweet juices from the convenience store.

Minerva The married woman in the neighborhood who is most similar to Esperanza. Minerva and Esperanza share their poems with each other. She is only two years older than Esperanza but already has a husband and two children. Her husband leaves for long periods, only to return in a violent rage.

Tito A neighborhood boy who relates to girls in violent and sexual ways. Tito flirts with Esperanza by pushing her in front of an open fire hydrant, and later he steals Sally's keys in order to get her to kiss him and his friends.

Sire Esperanza's first crush. Sire sometimes stares at Esperanza, and though she is afraid, she tries sometimes to look back at him. Sire and his girlfriend Lois hang around outside late at night. Esperanza's father tells her Sire is a punk, and Esperanza's mother tells her Lois is the kind of girl who will go with a boy into an alley.

Earl A neighbor who works nights and tries to sleep during the day. Earl sometimes brings women home with him for short periods. The neighbors see these women at different times, and each thinks a different woman is his wife, but the women are probably prostitutes.

The Three Sisters Old ladies Esperanza meets at Lucy and Rachel's baby sister's wake. The three sisters are mysterious and guess Esperanza's hopes and dreams. They advise Esperanza always to return to Mango Street after she leaves it.

ANALYSIS OF MAJOR CHARACTERS

ESPERANZA

As Esperanza matures during the year that makes up *The House on Mango Street*, she experiences a series of awakenings, the most important being a sexual awakening. At the beginning of the novel, Esperanza is not quite ready to emerge from the asexuality of childhood. She is completely ignorant about sex and says that boys and girls live in completely different worlds. She is so much a child that she cannot even speak to her brothers outside of the house. When she becomes an adolescent, she begins to experiment with the power she, as a young woman, has over men. Marin teaches her fundamental facts about boys, but the first major step in Esperanza's awareness of her sexuality is when she and her friends explore the neighborhood in high-heeled shoes. She relishes the power the shoes seem to give her, and she plays with the idea that physical beauty could help her escape the squalor of her surroundings. Esperanza quickly learns, however, that the patriarchal society in which she lives denies the power of female sexuality. The bum who attempts to kiss Rachel is the first in a series of men who will use force to take what girls don't want to give freely. After being sexually assaulted, Esperanza decides to try to forget some of what she has learned about sex in the past year in order to focus on writing. By the end of the novel, Esperanza's views on sex have evolved, and she rejects sex as a means of escape.

Esperanza's moral sense develops from an intense individualism to a feeling of responsibility toward the people in her community. As a child, Esperanza wants only to escape Mango Street. Her dreams of self-definition don't include the fact that she has any responsibility to her family or to the people around her, and she wishes to leave them all behind. Once Esperanza has become familiar with the people in her neighborhood, however, she begins to feel affection and, ultimately, responsibility for them. She no longer sees herself as an individual striving for self-determination. Instead, she recognizes herself as a member of a social network who must give back to her community in order to break the cycle of poverty that plagues the neighborhood. Esperanza also develops feelings of moral responsibility toward her community of women. Her negative experiences as Sally's friend show that she has the courage to try to help her friends, even if they do not always understand that they need to help her as well. Not until she talks with the three sisters and Alicia, however, does Esperanza understand that helping the neighborhood women will be a lifelong effort.

Esperanza's final and most important awakening is her realization of her writing ability, which gives her the means to escape from Mango Street. Because Esperanza is a writer, she is a keen observer, and we see her powers of observation mature. She is present in all of the early stories she narrates, but by the middle of the novel she is able to narrate stories based wholly on observation of the people around her. This change shows that she is becoming an artist, and also that she is becoming more detached from her neighborhood, since she does not always see herself in the stories she tells. By the end of *The House on Mango Street*, she knows she has become more detached from her home through her writing. Although she has not yet found a home of her own, her writing has helped her to find privacy within herself.

SALLY

When Esperanza begins desiring boys, she seeks out a friend in Sally, whom boys find desirable. Sally seems to be beautiful and cruel, like the women Esperanza admires in movies. She leans against the fence at school and doesn't talk to anyone. Rumors about Sally's promiscuity circulate, but Esperanza doesn't believe them. Instead, she thinks of Sally as a kindred spirit, someone who also spends her time dreaming of escaping the neighborhood. Sally, however, is not interested only in driving boys crazy and then laughing them away, as the women in the movies do. Instead, she finds safety and comfort in sex, feelings she does not find at home with her abusive father. Sally's sexual exploits make Esperanza uncomfortable, since at this point Esperanza is interested in sex only abstractly. Eventually, this discomfort becomes extreme, and Sally ends up putting Esperanza in physical danger. Sally herself changes little, but Esperanza's understanding of her changes dramatically. Esperanza's experiences as Sally's friend make Esperanza realize she has tried to mature too quickly. In the end, Sally is a pitiable, not enviable, figure in Esperanza's life.

NENNY

As the younger sister, Nenny is often Esperanza's responsibility, and though her innocence is a major source of annoyance for Esperanza, it also signals Nenny's independence. In many ways, Nenny is a pesky little sister. Esperanza must introduce Nenny to her new friends and keep her away from bad influences, such as the Vargas kids. Nenny also has qualities that Esperanza covets, including two names ("Nenny" is short for "Magdalena"), pretty eyes, and shiny, straight hair. Though Nenny can be a nuisance and a tag-a-long, and her actions often embarrass and annoy Esperanza, she frequently demonstrates her independence. When Esperanza, Rachel, and Lucy make up chants about hips, Nenny recites old chants that everyone already knows. Similarly, when Rachel and Lucy describe clouds with creative metaphors, Nenny gives the clouds everyday names such as Jose and Alicia. Nenny's apparent refusal to be creative embarrasses Esperanza, but her choices suggest she has her own way of surviving on Mango Street.

Nenny and Esperanza don't seem very much alike, but their differences in age and sociability mask their fundamental similarities. Nenny and Esperanza laugh at the same things, even those things others don't understand are funny. More important, Nenny and Esperanza are both dreamers. While Esperanza imagines a world outside the barrio, Nenny turns the outside world into the barrio by giving the clouds the same names as her neighbors. By doing so, she enlarges her world and makes it bearable. She turns Mango Street into the center of the universe, a place where she can be happy. Nenny and Esperanza are also very steadfast in their ideas, though Nenny is less likely to go along with the other girls if her views differ. While Esperanza, Lucy, and Rachel bounce ideas off each other, Nenny pursues her own idea. She is not distracted from her dreams, even when the other girls give her dirty looks. Despite Nenny's similarities to Esperanza, Nenny does not have as much a part in Esperanza's narrative as other women. Esperanza observes most of the women in her life closely and gives each of them a chapter—except for Nenny. Nenny ultimately recedes from view as Esperanza pursues life beyond Mango Street.

THEMES, MOTIFS, AND SYMBOLS

THEMES

Themes are the fundamental and often universal ideas explored in a literary work.

THE POWER OF LANGUAGE

Throughout *The House on Mango Street*, particularly in "No Speak English," those who are not able to communicate effectively (or at all) are relegated to the bottom levels of society. Mamacita moves to the country to be with her husband, and she becomes a prisoner of her apartment because she does not speak English. She misses home and listens to the Spanish radio station, and she is distraught when her baby begins learning English words. His new language excludes her. Similarly, Esperanza's father could not even choose what he ate when he first moved to the country, because he did not know the words for any of the foods but ham and eggs. Esperanza's mother may be a native English speaker, but her letter to the nuns at Esperanza's school is unconvincing to them in part because it is poorly written.

Esperanza observes the people around her and realizes that if not knowing or not mastering the language creates powerlessness, then having the ability to manipulate language will give her power. She wants to change her name so that she can have power over her own destiny. Her Aunt Lupe tells her to keep writing because it will keep her free, and Esperanza eventually understands what her aunt means. Writing keeps Esperanza spiritually free, because putting her experiences into words gives her power over them. If she can use beautiful language to write about a terrible experience, then the experience seems less awful. Esperanza's spiritual freedom may eventually give her the power to be literally free as well.

THE STRUGGLE FOR SELF-DEFINITION

The struggle for self-definition is a common theme in a coming-of-age novel, or bildungsroman, and in *The House on Mango Street*, Esperanza's struggle to define herself underscores her every action and encounter. Esperanza must define herself both as a woman and as an artist, and her perception of her identity changes over the course of the novel. In the beginning of the novel Esperanza wants to change her name so that she can define herself on her own terms, instead of accepting a name that expresses her family heritage. She wants to separate herself from her parents and her younger sister in order to create her own life, and changing her name seems to her an important step in that direction. Later, after she becomes more sexually aware, Esperanza would like to be "beautiful and cruel" so men will like her but not hurt her, and she pursues that goal by becoming friends with Sally. After she is assaulted, she doesn't want to define herself as "beautiful and cruel" anymore, and she is, once again, unsure of who she is.

Eventually, Esperanza decides she does not need to set herself apart from the others in her neighborhood or her family heritage by changing her name, and she stops forcing herself to develop sexually, which she isn't fully ready for. She accepts her place in her community and decides that the most important way she can define herself is as a writer. As a writer, she observes and interacts with the world in a way that sets her apart from non-writers, giving her the legitimate new identity she's been searching for. Writing promises to help her leave Mango Street emotionally, and possibly physically as well.

SEXUALITY VS. AUTONOMY

In *The House on Mango Street*, Esperanza's goals are clear: she wants to escape her neighborhood and live in a house of her own. These ambitions are always in her mind, but as she begins to mature, the desire for men appears in her thoughts as well. At first, the desire to escape and the desire for men don't seem mutually exclusive, but as Esperanza observes other women in the neighborhood and the marriages that bind them, she begins to doubt that she can pursue both. Most of the women Esperanza meets are either trapped in marriages that keep them on Mango Street or tied down by their children. Esperanza decides she does not want to be like these women, but her dire observations of married life do not erase her sexual yearnings for neighborhood boys.

Esperanza decides she'll combine sexuality with autonomy by being "beautiful and cruel" like Sally and the women in movies. However, Esperanza finds out that being "beautiful and cruel" is impossible in her male-dominated society when she experiences sexual assault. In her dreams about being with Sire, Esperanza is always in control, but in her encounter with the boys who assault her, she has no power whatsoever. The assault makes Esperanza realize that achieving true independence won't be possible if she pursues relationships with the men in her neighborhood. She puts aside her newfound sexual awareness, rejoins Lucy and Rachel, her less sexually mature friends, and spends her time concentrating on writing instead of on boys. She chooses, for the present, autonomy over sexuality, which gives her the best chance of escape.

WOMEN'S UNFULFILLED RESPONSIBILITIES TO EACH OTHER

Early in the novel, Esperanza says that boys and girls live in different worlds, and this observation proves true of men and women in every stage of life. Since the women's world is often isolating and grants women so little power, Esperanza feels women have a responsibility to protect and make life easier for each other. However, on Mango Street, this responsibility goes unfulfilled. The boys and men in *The House on Mango Street* are consistently violent, exploitative, or absent, but their world is so foreign to the women that no woman rebels against the men or calls for them to change. Esperanza may call out for women to help each other in the face of the unchanging male world, but no one answers.

Esperanza accepts more responsibility for women as she matures, and as she does, she confronts other women's indifference more directly. At first Esperanza is responsible only for her younger sister, Nenny, but her responsibilities grow when she befriends Sally. Esperanza tries to save Sally from having to kiss a group of boys in "The Monkey Garden." However, when Esperanza tries to enlist one of the boys' mothers to help her, the mother refuses. Later, Sally abandons Esperanza and leaves her vulnerable to male attackers in "Red Clowns." Esperanza expects female friends to protect each other, and Sally does not fulfill this responsibility. Ultimately, Esperanza understands that even if and when she leaves Mango Street, she will continue to take responsibility for the women in her neighborhood. She feels the responsibility deeply and will not forget it.

MOTIFS

MOTIFS

Motifs are recurring structures, contrasts, or literary devices that can help to develop and inform the text's major themes.

NAMES

Esperanza is one of the only characters in *The House on Mango Street* with just one name—most characters have two. Some have a real name and a nickname, such as Nenny, whose real name is Magdalena, and Aunt Lupe, whose real name is Guadeloupe. Others have an English name and a Spanish name, such as Meme Ortiz, whose Spanish name is Juan, and Meme's dog, which has unspecified names in both languages. These dual or multiple names emphasize the mix of cultures and languages that make up Esperanza's neighborhood and the difficulties her neighbors have in figuring out who they are, in their families, their neighborhood, even their country.

The power of names to transform and empower fascinates Esperanza, who struggles with how to define herself. She mentions the transforming power of names in "My Name," where she picks Zeze the X as a new name for herself. She also gives her current name, Esperanza, several definitions in order to make it more powerful. In "And Some More," Esperanza discusses the fact that the Eskimos have thirty names for snow. She speculates that the Eskimos have so many names for snow because snow is so important to them, which suggests that the more names a person has, the more important he or she is. Rachel rejoins by saying that her cousin has three last names and two first names, indicating that she, too, shares the theory that the more names one has, the better. Eventually, Esperanza places more importance on language and description than on naming alone, but her obsession with naming shows an early understanding of the importance of language.

FALLING

Throughout *The House on Mango Street*, people fear falling and sometimes actually fall, which suggests the constant threat of failure or injury. Images of falling appear frequently. Angel Vargas and Meme both fall from significant heights, both with disastrous results. Marin waits for a star to fall to change her life. Esperanza even describes herself as floating in an early vignette, as a red balloon on a tether. When she finally abandons her tether, she hopes she'll fly away and not fall to the ground as Angel and Meme did. Esperanza faces the same fear of falling her neighbors do, and she hopes for a different fate.

WOMEN BY WINDOWS

Mango Street is full of women who are trapped by their husbands, fathers, children, or their own feelings of inadequacy. Esperanza's long-dead great-grandmother married unwillingly and spent her

whole life sitting sadly by her window. Four women in Esperanza's neighborhood are trapped in their apartments—Mamacita, Rafaela, Minerva, and Sally. They sit by their windows all day and look down onto the street. The group makes up a kind of community, but these women cannot communicate, and each keeps to her place without much complaint. Esperanza is determined not to become a woman sitting by a window, and she understands there is something amiss among the women in her world. Eventually, she tries to help by supporting women when she can. For now, however, the women represent a disturbing failure: that of the more liberated women to help their confined and unhappy neighbors.

SYMBOLS

Symbols are objects, characters, figures, or colors used to represent abstract ideas or concepts.

SHOES

Shoes in *The House on Mango Street* frequently evoke images of sex and adult femininity, and for Esperanza they illustrate the conflict she feels between her emerging sexual attractiveness and her desire for independence. Esperanza makes the connection between shoes and sex for the first time when she, Lucy, and Rachel try on high-heeled shoes a neighbor gives them. The shoes transform their scarred, childish feet and legs into long, slim women's legs, and what began as a childhood game of dress-up becomes something more dangerous, as male neighbors ogle them hungrily. That afternoon, they are happy to abandon the shoes, claiming they are bored with them. For the moment, Esperanza can smoothly shed her new sexual attractiveness and become a child again.

When shoes appear again, Esperanza can't discard them so easily. When Esperanza attends a dance and wears brown saddle shoes with her pretty new dress, she is almost paralyzed with embarrassment and self-consciousness. Men ask her to dance, and she wants to dance, but she wants more to hide her worn-out little-girl shoes. Though she eventually dances with her uncle and relishes the stares of a boy, she is aware of her clunky shoes the entire time. When Esperanza wants to befriend Sally, who is sexually mature, she describes Sally's black suede shoes and wonders if she can convince her mother to buy her a similar pair. When Sally abandons Esperanza in the monkey garden in order to fool around with boys, Esperanza thinks her own feet look foreign. Finally, in Esperanza's vision of her dream house, her shoes are beside the bed, suggesting that she does have or will have some measure of control over her own sexuality, if only in her imagination.

TREES

Esperanza expresses respect and admiration for trees throughout *The House on Mango Street*, and her affection stems from her identification with their appearance, resilience, and independence. In "Four Skinny Trees," Esperanza personifies the trees in her front yard, saying she and they understand each other, even that they teach her things. She relates to the trees because they don't seem to belong in the neighborhood and because they persevere despite the concrete that tries to keep them in the ground. Esperanza herself does not seem to belong, and she plans to persevere despite the obstacles posed by her poor neighborhood. Esperanza views the trees almost as a reflection of herself, comparing her own skinny neck and pointy elbows to the tree's spindly branches.

The tree in Meme Ortiz's backyard has particular resonance for Esperanza. Even though the tree eventually turns out to be dangerous, since Meme jumps out of it and breaks both of his arms, Esperanza claims it is the most memorable part of Meme's backyard. She points out that the tree is full of squirrels and that it dwarfs her neighborhood in age and size. This tree has flourished even more than the trees in her front yard have, again without anybody doing much to help it. Meme's hardy tree was probably once like the elms in Esperanza's yard, which suggests that Esperanza will perhaps be able to grow into a strong and independent woman despite the setbacks in her first year on Mango Street.

POETRY

The House on Mango Street contains many small poems and references to poems, which emphasize the importance of language to Esperanza and her neighbors. These references and poems include a poem Esperanza writes, jump-roping chants, and simple, internal rhymes within paragraphs of the text. We never hear some of the poems, such as those Esperanza recites to Ruthie, or those Minerva writes. The abundance of poetry suggests that the women and girls on Mango Street try to make their lives better by describing the world with beautiful language. The novel itself, with its many internal rhymes, is in some ways Esperanza's long poem, her attempt to make some of the unpoetic aspects of her life less hard and more ordered through poetry.

Summary and Analysis

Sections 1–4

In English my name means hope. In Spanish it means too many letters. It means sadness, it means waiting.

(See QUOTATIONS, *p. 49*)

SUMMARY: "THE HOUSE ON MANGO STREET"
Esperanza describes how her family came to live at the house on Mango Street. She, her parents, her brothers, Carlos and Kiki, and her sister, Nenny, moved to Mango Street when the pipes broke in their previous apartment and the landlord refused to fix them. Before they moved into the house on Mango Street, the family moved around a lot. The family had dreamed of a white house with lots of space and bathrooms, but the house on Mango Street has only one bedroom and one bathroom. Esperanza notes that this is not the house that she envisioned, and although her parents tell her it's only temporary, she doubts they'll move anytime soon. The house, however, does have some significant advantages over the family's previous apartments. The family owns this house, so they are no longer subject to the whims of landlords, and at the old apartment, a nun made Esperanza feel ashamed about where she lived. The house on Mango Street is an improvement, but it is still not the house that Esperanza wants to point out as hers.

SUMMARY: "HAIRS"
Esperanza describes the different types of hair of all the members of her family. Her own hair doesn't do what she wants it to do, while her sister's is smooth and oily. Her mother's hair is beautiful and smells like bread. Esperanza likes to sleep near her mother so she can smell it.

SUMMARY: "BOYS AND GIRLS"
Esperanza notes that boys and girls do not socialize with each other in the neighborhood. Even though she can talk to her brothers at home, they refuse to talk to her outside. Esperanza must socialize with her younger sister Nenny, who, Esperanza notes, is too young and would not be her choice for a friend if she were not her sister. Worse, Nenny is Esperanza's responsibility. Esperanza has to make

sure that Nenny does not play with the Vargas kids. Esperanza longs for a best friend. Without one she compares herself to a "red balloon tied to an anchor."

Summary: "My Name"

We learn the narrator's name, Esperanza, for the first time. Esperanza muses on the meanings of her name, but she does so in a random, nonsensical way that we are not meant to take seriously. In English, she reflects, her name means "hope," while in Spanish it means "too many letters" as well as "sadness" and "waiting." She likes the way her name is pronounced in Spanish, but not in English.

Esperanza is named after her great-grandmother, and both she and her great-grandmother were born in the Chinese year of the horse. The horse is an animal that represents strength, and being born under this sign is supposed to be bad luck for women. Esperanza rejects this superstition, explaining that she believes both the Chinese and the Mexicans discourage women from being strong. Esperanza never met her great-grandmother, but she compares her to a wild horse. She did not want to get married but was forced into marriage and never forgave her husband. She spent her life gazing sadly out the window. Esperanza says that while she has inherited her great-grandmother's name, she does not want to "inherit her place by the window."

Esperanza would like to change her name to one that expresses her true self. She lists several possible choices, settling eventually on Zeze the X.

Analysis

The first sections of *The House on Mango Street* introduce Esperanza's storytelling style. Cisneros calls these short chapters "lazy poems," because, like many poems, the chapters are short, do not tell full stories, and rely on the sounds of words for added meaning or emphasis. Some of the stories are just series of observations, while others contain more complete scenes. The short chapters also reflect the short attention span of a young girl, and this storytelling technique seems appropriate considering Esperanza's age. Esperanza has not really learned how to tell stories correctly, and she relies on fragments that are grouped together loosely. The chapters are only tenuously connected, and an element of one often triggers another observation in the next. In "The House on Mango Street," Esperanza complains that the house has only one bedroom, while in

"Hairs" she explains what it's like to sleep in that bedroom with her whole family. Describing her siblings' hair then reminds her that she cannot talk to her brothers outside the house, and "Boys and Girls" follows. The entire novel continues this way, with both random and not so random connections and logic.

Esperanza does not introduce herself by name, while other novels that depend on a first person voice, such as *Moby-Dick* or *David Copperfield*, have narrators who introduce themselves immediately. When the narrators of *Moby-Dick* or *David Copperfield* name themselves, they are announcing that they have a sense of identity and that they will reveal, in retrospect, the story of how they came to be who they are. *The House on Mango Street* resembles James Joyce's *A Portrait of the Artist as a Young Man*, in which the narrator offers fragmented observations and is still involved in the process of finding a coherent sense of self, thus giving the reader a more immediate view of childhood experience. Esperanza tells her own story through vignettes, each of which reveals a bit more of who she is and who she wants to be. She observes the people around her and reflects on her experiences, but she does not connect them in a way that suggests she understands their greater meaning in her life. She is too young, and too involved, to narrate objectively, and we must piece together her stories. Esperanza matures throughout the novel, and by the end she has gained a clearer sense of who she is. In the final vignette, "Mango Says Goodbye Sometimes," she says she likes to tell stories, which indicates that she is beginning to identify herself as a writer. Ultimately, she moves toward an understanding of how her experiences have affected her and how they will continue to influence her as she gets older.

Esperanza's great-grandmother, also named Esperanza, is the first of many women who are trapped by men, society, and their own sense of defeat. The elder Esperanza was initially a strong woman, but after her forced marriage she spent most of her days sitting by a window. Windows appear frequently in situations similar to the elder Esperanza's, suggesting that these trapped women do not accept their cages blindly but instead are always aware of the world outside that is off-limits to them. Esperanza demonstrates her own awareness of the larger world when she observes that being born in the year of the horse isn't necessarily bad luck, but that the Mexicans and Chinese don't like their women to be strong like horses. Esperanza is just a young girl from the barrio, hardly knowledgeable enough to generalize about the Chinese, and her observation suggests wisdom beyond her years. Most likely Esperanza heard such a theory from her mother or one of the other *mujeres*, or women, surrounding her.

The first few sections of *The House on Mango Street* suggest that Esperanza will focus on the importance and experiences of her family, but this focus eventually expands. Esperanza's family and house fill these first few sections, so specifically that Esperanza even discusses the security she finds in the smell of her mother's hair. However, the introduction of the family is only an introduction to what will become Esperanza's larger family, the barrio. She may find comfort in her mother's hair, but Esperanza does not actually mention her mother again for another thirty-five sections. Although the novel begins narrowly, with the immediate family and house as subjects, Mango Street itself, with its larger community, eventually occupies Esperanza's life, with home and family constituting only the starting point.

> *Until then I am a red balloon, a balloon tied to an anchor.*
>
> *(See* QUOTATIONS, *p. 50)*

SECTIONS 5–8

SUMMARY: "CATHY QUEEN OF CATS"
Cathy becomes Esperanza's first friend in her new neighborhood. Cathy claims to be related to the queen of France and hopes to go to France someday to inherit the family house. She tells Esperanza about the other people on Mango Street and disparages nearly all of them. She agrees to be Esperanza's friend only for a week, until next Tuesday, when her family will move. She offends Esperanza by telling her that her family is moving because the neighborhood is getting bad, when clearly what makes it bad is that families like Esperanza's are moving in.

SUMMARY: "OUR GOOD DAY"
Esperanza sacrifices her friendship with Cathy by pitching in for a bike that she will share with her two new friends, Lucy and Rachel. Cathy does not want Esperanza to have anything to do with Lucy and Rachel, explaining that they "smell like a broom." Lucy and Rachel are Chicana sisters whose family is from Texas, and they are more similar to Esperanza than Cathy is. Esperanza is embarrassed

to tell her new friends her name, but they don't laugh at it or find it unusual. Esperanza knows she eventually must share her friends and bike with her sister Nenny, since she took money from Nenny to help pay for the bike, but for now, she decides to wait and keep her new friends to herself. The three girls ride their new bike together around the block, and Esperanza describes the geography of the neighborhood.

SUMMARY: "LAUGHTER"
Esperanza explains that although she and Nenny do not look alike as Lucy and Rachel do, they do have a lot in common. They laugh in the same, loud way, and sometimes they have the same ideas. One day Esperanza sees a house that reminds her of houses in Mexico, although she can't say exactly why. Rachel and Lucy laugh at her, but Nenny tells them she was thinking the same thing as Esperanza.

SUMMARY: "GIL'S FURNITURE BOUGHT & SOLD"
In Esperanza's neighborhood, an old black man runs a junk store, and he doesn't turn on the lights unless he knows his customers have money. Esperanza and Nenny wander around the store in the dark. The store is labyrinthine and full of mysterious items, as well as piles of broken televisions. This is the store where Esperanza's family bought their refrigerator when they moved into the neighborhood. Esperanza is afraid to talk to the owner and only does so when she buys a little Statue of Liberty. Nenny is not intimidated by him, and one day she asks him about a wooden box in the shop. It is a music box, and the man plays it for them. Esperanza finds the music surprising and emotional. Nenny tries to buy the box, but the man tells her it's not for sale.

SUMMARY: "MEME ORTIZ"
Meme, whose real name is Juan, and his dog, who has both English and Spanish names, move into Cathy's house after her family leaves the neighborhood. Esperanza describes the house, a wooden house Cathy's father built. It has a tree in the backyard that is taller than Esperanza's house. When the kids had a Tarzan jumping contest, Meme jumped out of the tree and broke both his arms.

ANALYSIS
These chapters paint a geographical and cultural picture from both the past and the present of Mango Street and the surrounding neighborhood. Cathy indicates what the neighborhood may have been

like in the past, while the two families that move into her house once she's left are more representative of the whole neighborhood as Esperanza comes to experience it. The black man who owns Gil's furniture is an aberration from the rest of the neighborhood, different from the people Esperanza sees from day to day. His race makes him so unfamiliar that Esperanza is afraid to talk to him. Meme and his dog each have two names, a fact that highlights the neighborhood's two cultures, Latin American and American, and two languages, Spanish and English, revealing the new cultural makeup of Mango Street. When Esperanza bikes around the neighborhood with Lucy and Rachel, she reveals its physical limitations. She points out her house again as rundown, and the neighborhood seems no better. Mango Street is near a dangerous busy street, and her house is still near a laundromat. The laundromat is reminiscent of the laundromat below the apartment where Esperanza used to live. That one was boarded up because it was robbed, and it was a keen source of embarrassment for Esperanza. That her new house is also near a laundromat suggests that the move to Mango Street is far from enough to change her circumstances.

Cathy provides a window into how outsiders view Esperanza's neighborhood, even though Cathy is blind to her own family's similarities to the families around them. Cathy's family is moving because the neighborhood is "getting bad," a racist reason that Esperanza immediately understands. Esperanza's immigrant family, as well as other families like hers, is, in Cathy's family's view, causing the neighborhood to deteriorate, and the only thing to do is move. However, Cathy's family does not seem to be struggling any less than the other families in Esperanza's neighborhood. Their house, which Cathy's father built, is overrun with cats and has dangerously crooked wooden stairs, no less an eyesore than any other house around them. Cathy, much like Esperanza, has created a world full of dreams and imagination to survive, and she tries to demonstrate her superiority to Esperanza by lying about being the queen of France. Though Cathy does not make racist comments explicitly about Esperanza, Esperanza understands that the comments apply to her, and she describes Cathy as rude. She sees clearly that families like Cathy's will have to keep moving further away as families like Esperanza's keep moving in.

In Lucy and Rachel, Esperanza finds the friends she's been yearning for, but they do not prove to be the kinds of friends with whom she can share her deepest secrets, or who will support her in difficult times. In "Boys and Girls," Esperanza longs for a friend. She points out that you can't choose your sister, implying that she isn't happy spending her time with or sharing her secrets with Nenny. However, when Esperanza does find friends, she finds in "Laughter" that Nenny sometimes understands her better than her friends do. This surprising revelation suggests that although Esperanza is willing to share her story, she won't be able to share everything with the other young women in her life. She'll have to go through the process of growing up almost entirely on her own.

SECTIONS 9–13

She looked out the window her whole life, the way so many women sit their sadness on an elbow. I wonder if she made the best with what she got or was she sorry because she couldn't be all the things she wanted to be. Esperanza. I have inherited her name, but I don't want to inherit her place by the window.

(See QUOTATIONS, p. 51)

SUMMARY: "LOUIE, HIS COUSIN & HIS OTHER COUSIN"
Meme Ortiz's family rents their basement apartment to a Puerto Rican family. The family's son Louie is a friend of Esperanza's brother. Louie's cousin Marin also lives with the family in the basement. Marin is older than Esperanza and wears nylons and Avon makeup, which she also sells in her free time. She sings sassy songs about boyfriends while she baby-sits Louie's little sisters. One day, another cousin of Louie's drives up in a beautiful new Cadillac and takes the neighborhood kids for a ride. They go around the block again and again, until they hear sirens. Louie's cousin orders everyone out and takes off in the car. He doesn't quite make the turn at the end of the alley, though, and crashes into a streetlight. The cops arrest him.

SUMMARY: "MARIN"
Louie's cousin Marin has a boyfriend in Puerto Rico whom she plans to marry when she goes back. At the same time, she hopes to stay in Chicago next year so she can get a job downtown. She hopes to meet a rich man on the subway who will marry her and take her to live outside the barrio. She tells Esperanza and her friends useful things like how girls get pregnant and how to remove unwanted facial hair, as well as girlish superstitions, such as how the number of calcium deposits on their fingernails corresponds with the number of boys who like them. She spends her days baby-sitting Louie's sisters,

and in the evening, she takes her radio outside and dances, smokes cig-arettes, and waits for boys to come by. Esperanza notes that she does not seem afraid of the boys. The section ends with a description of Marin in the future somewhere else. She is still dancing under a stree-tlight, waiting for a man to swoop down and change her life.

SUMMARY: "THOSE WHO DON'T"
Esperanza says that people "who don't know any better" think her neighborhood is dangerous, and that if they find themselves in it at night, they fear they'll get stabbed. Esperanza and her friends are never scared in the neighborhood, since they know the people out-siders might find frightening, including the man with the crooked eye, the tall intimidating man in the hat, and a large retarded man. However, Esperanza notes that when she enters a non-Chicano eth-nic neighborhood, she herself gets scared.

SUMMARY: "THERE WAS AN OLD WOMAN SHE HAD SO MANY CHILDREN SHE DIDN'T KNOW WHAT TO DO"
Esperanza describes the Vargas kids, whom she described earlier as being bad. They have a single mother, Rosa Vargas, who is over-whelmed by and unable to control her many children, and who is still sad about the fact that their father left her without a note or any money to help. The children don't care about themselves or any-body else. At first the people in the neighborhood feel bad for the children and try to make them stop misbehaving, but eventually the people become tired of trying and stop caring. They don't care when the children hurt themselves, even when Angel Vargas falls from a great height and dies.

ANALYSIS
Esperanza manages to chronicle the passing of time in these and other sections, even though, on the surface, the stories seem to be independent, unconnected incidents. At the beginning of *The House on Mango Street*, Esperanza meets Cathy, who agrees to be her friend only until Tuesday, and then she meets Lucy and Rachel sometime within that week. The section about Meme takes place soon after Cathy's family moves out, and then Louie's family moves into the basement apartment in that house about a month later. Esperanza's year in the house on Mango Street is already well under-way, without her ever having explicitly noted that time has passed. Since these new characters—Meme, Louie, Louie's other cousin, Marin, the Vargas kids—appear in only one or two sections, Esper-

anza must tell their stories in the past, present, and future. Meme probably doesn't break his arms during his first week in the house, for example, and in the section about the Vargas kids, Esperanza shows an evolution of the neighborhood's attitudes toward the kids, from caring and pity to apathy. The incidents Esperanza describes take place at any time during the year, and Marin's section even moves into the future, beyond what Esperanza can really know.

These sections contain many images of people who try to fly and cannot quite make it. Angel Vargas and Meme both fall from great heights. Angel is trying to fly, and Meme is trying to be Tarzan, both with disastrous results. Similarly, Marin is waiting for a star to fall from the sky to change her life. The children's efforts to fly suggest their efforts to escape their current situations in the world—Angel is trying to fly away while Meme is looking for a life of adventure. Marin hopes the star that will fall will be a man who will bring her back up with him. Esperanza has previously described herself as a red balloon on a tether. When she finally abandons her tether, she'd like to fly away, not fall to the ground, but her future is at this point uncertain.

In "Marin," Esperanza does not mention herself when she describes Marin, just as she doesn't mention herself when she profiles other women in other vignettes. In this way, Esperanza is only a silent observer, looking for role models to take from this group of slightly older women, and Marin indeed tries to be a role model. She teaches the girls the basics about relationships between men and women. As glamorous as Marin seems with her makeup and her confidence around boys, Esperanza knows Marin will eventually fail. Instead of working at a department store downtown as she imagines, her cousins will send her back to Puerto Rico after she baby-sits for a year. Esperanza can see that Marin is a dreamer and that she has neither a definite goal nor any control over her own destiny. On the one hand, Marin thinks it is romantic to have a secret fiancé back home, but in Chicago she looks for someone to sweep her off her feet. Esperanza knows Marin will always be looking for someone else to save her, "a falling star," instead of trying to change herself. Esperanza differentiates herself from Marin by trying to be single-minded in her goal of leaving the neighborhood.

In "Those Who Don't," Esperanza explores racism more directly than in any other section. Esperanza understands that some people in her neighborhood would indeed frighten an outsider, such as the people with physical or mental handicaps who stand on the street. However, the neighborhood children know these strange people's families and histories, so they are not afraid. Esperanza takes comfort in knowing these family connections, but she also mentions that they are "all brown all around," which suggests that racial familiarity and similarity also keep her unafraid in her own neighborhood. She is afraid to be in black or Asian neighborhoods, but for her the problem is her lack of knowledge, not hardened prejudice. Esperanza's neighborhood isn't completely harmless, however. In "Louie, His Cousin & His Other Cousin," Louie's other cousin has either stolen the car he drives or has bought it with money from another crime. He shows a darker aspect of the barrio: sometimes men try to escape through a life of crime, which, as Louie's other cousin shows, is not always successful.

SECTIONS 14–17

SUMMARY: "ALICIA WHO SEES MICE"
Alicia is a neighborhood girl whose mother has died. She must do all the cooking and cleaning for her father. Alicia is also trying to attend college, traveling far on public transportation every day so she can escape a life of domestic toil. She stays up all night studying and thus sees the mice that come out at night. Her father gives her a hard time about her studies. He says the mice don't exist and that a woman's job is to get up early to make tortillas for her younger siblings' lunches.

SUMMARY: "DARIUS AND THE CLOUDS"
Esperanza complains about living in the inner city, saying there is not enough sky or flowers or butterflies. Yet the children in the neighborhood make the best of what they have. One day, when the sky is full of puffy clouds that everyone is admiring, Darius, a boy Esperanza doesn't like because he tries to be tough, says something Esperanza finds wise: he looks up at a particular cloud and calls it God.

SUMMARY: "AND SOME MORE"
A conversation about clouds between Esperanza, Nenny, Lucy, and Rachel turns into a fight. Esperanza says the Eskimos have thirty different names for snow, which leads them into a discussion about names for clouds. Esperanza knows two names: cumulus and nimbus. She is concerned with the actual names, while Nenny makes up lists of everyday names, such as Lisa and Ted. Nenny does this throughout the story and refuses to respond to her sister or to her friends while they are fighting. Rachel and Lucy are more interested in what the clouds are similar to in their everyday lives, like hair

after it's been brushed or their friend's fat face. One of the girls says Esperanza has an ugly fat face, and after this the girls playfully exchange creative insults.

SUMMARY: "THE FAMILY OF LITTLE FEET"

Esperanza imagines a family of people with tiny, plump feet. Her description of the fairy-tale family merges into an account of a day when a woman gives her, Nenny, Rachel, and Lucy some old pairs of high-heeled shoes that happen to fit their small feet perfectly. The girls are amazed at these shoes because when they put them on, they suddenly have attractive, womanly legs. Some of their male neighbors warn them that such suggestive shoes are not meant for little girls, but the girls ignore them. Other men tease them with sexual comments. The shoes cause a flirtation between Rachel and a drunken bum. He asks her to kiss him for a dollar. Frightened, Lucy leads the girls back to Mango Street. They hide the shoes on Rachel and Lucy's porch, and later Rachel and Lucy's mother throws them away. The girls are glad the shoes are gone.

ANALYSIS

Though Cathy introduced Alicia in an earlier section as having gotten snobby since she went to college, here we see that Cathy's description is inaccurate. Alicia isn't snobby—she's busy. She is struggling to fulfill the responsibilities of a full-time mother while trying to get an education. Her father faults her for not working enough for the family, and the neighborhood calls her "stuck-up," but she is actually striving for self-improvement. The patriarchal nature of Hispanic society poses a problem for girls with ambitions, such as Alicia and Esperanza. In these families, when the mother dies, the oldest female child, not the father, takes over responsibility for raising the children, which is why Alicia wishes there were someone older to do the work. To escape her situation, Alicia has chosen to pursue an education, much different from Marin's or Louie's other cousin's escape routes. Alicia does not have the support of her family or the community, which means she'll have a difficult time overcoming a sexist tradition. Because Alicia is the character most similar to Esperanza so far, her struggles suggest that Esperanza, too, will have difficulty asserting and achieving her independence.

Darius is the first boy Esperanza encounters who has poetic instincts similar to hers. This chapter is closer to a poem than any of the chapters so far. It contains many repeated words and internal rhymes: the word *sky* appears four times in the first paragraph, and the rhyming *school* and *fool* appear in the second. Though Esperanza lists Darius's transgressions, including chasing girls with firecrackers and a stick he says has touched a rat, she can't help expressing admiration for Darius's explanation that a single cloud is God. She is surprised that such a profound observation could come from a boy like Darius. Cisneros gives the impression that Darius may be forced by society into acting tough. Just as Esperanza does, he has his own way of coping with the barrio, necessarily different from Esperanza's way because he is a boy. However, he too has the ability to be poetic and wise despite his circumstances.

Darius and Esperanza are not the only poets in the neighborhood, and in "And Some More," the poetic natures of the other children become clear as they observe and describe clouds. Lucy, Rachel, and Nenny also make poetic observations, showing that Esperanza is not the only one who can make surprising comparisons. In fact, in this section we hear Esperanza's real voice, the voice she uses when she talks to her friends, instead of just her written voice. "And Some More" is a conversation, and, just as in "My Name," naming is a form of creativity. Lucy and Rachel compare clouds to everyday objects, while Nenny lists a string of people's names for the clouds. Esperanza is the only one of the girls occupied with the official Latin names for the clouds, and her schoolgirl attitude separates her from her friends. Her interest in the official names reveals her desire to pursue knowledge beyond what she can glean by living day to day.

Marin has tried to teach Esperanza and her friends to be confident and powerful in their encounters with boys, but "The Family of Little Feet" reveals the dangers sex and womanhood hold for these young girls. The shoes turn them magically into women, but at this point the girls are more interested in safety than sex, and they are too timid to fully express their newfound attractiveness. The sexual attractiveness they do express makes them vulnerable, and men like the bum show them that sexual power is not always as innocent or safe as it seems when Marin wields it. The bum offers money for a kiss, but the older girls suspect he might just as easily take what he offers to pay for. He is the first to hint that the sexual power that women like Marin seem so proud of may be just a myth. After being leered at and propositioned by the bum and other men, the girls are happy to abandon their put-on sexuality by leaving the shoes in a bag on the porch.

SECTIONS 18–21

SUMMARY: "A RICE SANDWICH"

Esperanza envies the kids who get to eat lunch in the canteen at school instead of having to go home for lunch. She pesters her mother to write her a note giving her permission to eat at the canteen and to pack her a lunch. Her mother is reluctant at first, but after it becomes clear that none of the other kids will need bag lunches, she writes a note for Esperanza and packs her a sandwich, one made of rice since the family cannot afford lunch meats. At school, Sister Superior does not accept Esperanza's mother's note, saying that Esperanza lives too close to school and must go home to eat. The Sister points to some rundown tenements up the street, accusing Esperanza of living there. Esperanza is embarrassed and nods her head, even though the buildings the nun points to are much more rundown than her own house. She gets to eat at the canteen that day but is too upset to enjoy the experience.

SUMMARY: "CHANCLAS"

For Esperanza's cousin's baptism, Esperanza's mother buys her a beautiful new outfit but forgets to buy the shoes that go with it. At the party after the baptism, Esperanza refuses to dance because she is embarrassed by her old brown saddle shoes. Her Uncle Nacho insists she is beautiful, and the two of them do a fancy new dance while everyone watches and applauds. Esperanza is proud that one particular boy watches her dance.

SUMMARY: "HIPS"

Esperanza, Nenny, Lucy, and Rachel jump rope and discuss the meaning of the hips they are beginning to develop. Rachel says that hips are good for propping a baby on while cooking, but Esperanza thinks this idea is unimaginative. Lucy says that hips are for dancing, while Nenny, who is too young to understand what it's like to develop hips, says that without them, you might turn into a man. Esperanza defends Nenny, then tries to give a scientific explanation about the purpose of hips that she gleaned from Alicia. Esperanza begins to believe hips have a musical quality. Rachel, Lucy, and Esperanza make up original chants about hips while dancing and jumping rope. Nenny repeats a rhyme she already knows, embarrassing Esperanza with her childishness.

SUMMARY: "THE FIRST JOB"

Esperanza's family wants her to get a summer job. She has been spending her days playing in the street and plans to begin looking sometime in the near future. One day, when she comes home after she lets a boy push her into the water from the open fire hydrant, she discovers that her aunt has found her a job matching pictures with negatives at the local photofinishing store. Esperanza just has to show up and lie about her age. The actual work is easy, but the social aspects of the job are difficult for Esperanza. She doesn't know whether she can sit down. She eats her lunch in the bathroom and takes her break in the coatroom. In the afternoon, a man Esperanza describes as older and Oriental befriends her. Esperanza feels more comfortable now that she has someone to eat lunch with. He asks her to give him a kiss because it's his birthday, but when Esperanza leans over to kiss him on the cheek he grabs her face and kisses her hard on the lips for a long time.

ANALYSIS

Esperanza experiences shame and embarrassment so acutely in these sections that the feelings nearly paralyze her. When she wants to eat at school, the nun makes her feel ashamed about where she lives—the second time a nun has demeaned Esperanza this way. In "Chanclas," which means "sandal," Esperanza's immense shame at her clunky school shoes keeps her from enjoying the party. When Esperanza has her first job, she is embarrassed because she doesn't know whether to stand up or sit down, and her shame leads her to scarf down her lunch in the bathroom. In all three of these situations, Esperanza's shame is largely self-imposed. People do not try to make Esperanza feel bad. Even in her experience with the nun, who does try to embarrass her, Esperanza ultimately exiles herself out of shame once she gets to the canteen. These sections suggest that, to succeed, Esperanza must overcome not only the obstacles society sets up, but also the stumbling block of her own feelings of shame.

"A Rice Sandwich" and "Hips" reveal the often vast differences between spoken and written language, or, in other words, public and private voices. In "A Rice Sandwich," we can hear Esperanza's mother's written voice in her note to the nun. Esperanza is ashamed of the note, which is not written convincingly enough to make the nun follow its instructions. The writing is stilted and childish, much different from the dynamic style in which Esperanza writes, and the voice of Esperanza's mother that we hear in the writing differs from other playful neighborhood voices. Esperanza has her own short-comings in the voice she shares with others. The voice Esperanza uses with her friends is neither as lyrical nor as interesting as her written voice. In "Hips," Esperanza expresses greater interest in the scientific explanation for hips than in the more creative, everyday uses her friends suggest, just as in "And Some More" Esperanza concerns herself with the actual names for clouds.

In these four sections, Esperanza begins to welcome her emerging sexual identity, but a forced kiss makes her anxious and wary of it. In "Chanclas," she is proud that one particular boy watches her dance. In "Hips," Esperanza's is the only jump-roping rhyme that explicitly expresses a desire for hips. In the beginning of "The First Job," Esperanza comes home wet because she has let a boy push her into the water flowing out of an open fire hydrant, the first sign of any outright flirting. However, this seemingly healthy and normal course of sexual maturity derails at the end of that section, when Esperanza's friendly peck on the cheek turns into a violent kiss on the mouth that is forced on her by an older man. Here, sexuality brings about violence, while in the previous two sections it was celebrated with dances and poetry.

SECTIONS 22–25

SUMMARY: "PAPA WHO WAKES UP TIRED IN THE DARK"
Esperanza's father tells her that her grandfather, or *abuelito*, has died. He cries, which is astounding for Esperanza to see. He will have to go to Mexico for the funeral, and Esperanza will have to explain to her younger siblings that they will not be able to play or go out today. Esperanza tries to imagine what it would be like if her father, who wakes up every morning before sunrise to go to work, died. She holds her father in her arms.

SUMMARY: "BORN BAD"
Esperanza and her friends Rachel and Lucy pray for themselves because they played a game that made fun of Esperanza's Aunt Lupe just before she died. Aunt Lupe was a strong and beautiful swimmer in her youth, but for all of Esperanza's life, she was bedridden and sick. The game consisted of the girls imitating someone they all knew. They usually imitated famous people, but one day they picked Lupe. Although Esperanza was afraid to visit Lupe, she liked her. She would bring library books and read to Lupe, and one day

she whispered one of her own poems in Lupe's ear. Aunt Lupe told Esperanza that she should keep writing because it would keep her free. Out on the schoolyard it was different, and Esperanza and her friends took turns imitating Lupe, not knowing she would die the next day. For this transgression, Esperanza believes she will go to hell.

SUMMARY: "ELENITA, CARDS, PALM, WATER"

Esperanza has her fortune told at the house of Elenita, a witch woman. Elenita seems very much like the other women in the neighborhood, except that she is somewhat better off. She is home with her two kids and has covered her sofas with plastic so the baby won't dirty them. She tries to get Esperanza to see something in a glass of water, but Esperanza can't really concentrate or believe in the spirits. Esperanza pays more attention to the Bugs Bunny cartoon in the background. Elenita puts out the Tarot cards and sees jealousy, sorrow, and luxury. Esperanza just wants to know whether Elenita sees a house in her future, but Elenita sees only a house of the heart. Esperanza pays Elenita five dollars and goes home disappointed.

SUMMARY: "GERALDO NO LAST NAME"

Marin meets a young man named Geraldo at a dance and dances with him a few times. After they leave the dance hall, a car strikes Geraldo, who speaks no English. He dies in the emergency room because no doctors come to help him. Marin has stayed with him at the hospital, although she does not know why. She has to answer the police's questions, but she can't tell them much. She doesn't even know Geraldo's last name. Esperanza imagines Geraldo's life—a series of run-down apartments and demeaning jobs to send money back home to Mexico. She also imagines the people in Geraldo's community in Mexico, who will wonder what became of him and will not know he is dead.

ANALYSIS

In "Papa Who Wakes Up Tired in the Dark," Esperanza empathizes with her father for the first time. She tries to put herself in her father's shoes by imagining what it would be like if her own father died. Previously, Esperanza has empathized with people only implicitly, and all of the people whose lives she has tried to imagine, such as Marin and Alicia, have been women. Esperanza's grandfather's death brings her face to face with her father's emotions for the first time. This section also marks the first time Esperanza must act as a parent. Since her father goes to Mexico for the funeral, Esperanza must explain the death to her siblings and keep discipline. While Alicia had to take the role of her mother, Esperanza takes over for her father. This subversion of gender roles foreshadows Esperanza's future rejection of her role as a woman in her own house.

Until "Born Bad," Esperanza has enjoyed writing and wanted to leave the neighborhood, but she never made the connection between the two desires. Aunt Lupe broaches the idea that Esperanza might be able to use the first to achieve the second. Lupe is the first person in *The House on Mango Street* to strongly support Esperanza's writing. Lupe doesn't compliment Esperanza after hearing her recite a poem, but instead tells her to keep writing because it "will keep [her] free." In the poem Esperanza recites for Lupe, Esperanza writes that she would like to jump out of her skin and shake the sky. Lupe resembles many seers and prophets from ancient mythology. She is blind, but she is wise and prophetic. Yet like most seers, she is ignored and mocked while she is alive. The girls are uncomfortable in her smelly apartment and play games in which they imitate her. Only after her death does Esperanza look back upon her as having been wise.

Aunt Lupe is a real fortuneteller, with an accurate prescription for escaping the barrio: hard work. Esperanza, however, wants an easier answer, so she sees a fortuneteller, Elenita, to ask if a house is in her future. Elenita's methods are a mixture of Catholic and pagan tradition, and though Esperanza wants to believe them, she can't. Her skepticism saves her from disappointment when Elenita gives her an ambiguous message, and it gives her the freedom to realize the prudence of Aunt Lupe's advice to determine her own fate. Esperanza's continued fascination with a home of her own has been strengthened by the deaths in her family and her difficulties at work. Elenita offers her the quickest way to get a home for herself, a home that will perhaps be more secure than any other kind, although Esperanza does not realize it. "A home in the heart" would be self-generated and thus inviolable and private, safe from sexual threats and the criticism of people like the nuns. Because she has not yet reached artistic or emotional maturity, though, Esperanza is not able to accept the idea of such a home, let alone construct one.

Sections 26–29

Summary: "Edna's Ruthie"

Ruthie is the grown-up daughter of Edna, a mean and exploitative landlord who owns the apartment building next door to Esperanza's house. One day when Angel Vargas is teaching them to whistle, Ruthie comes up and whistles beautifully. She likes to play with the children because she has never grown up enough to handle the adult world. She doesn't go into stores with the children, and one night when her mother's friends invite her to play bingo, she is paralyzed at the thought of going out with them. Ruthie is talented, but when she was young she got married instead of taking a job. Now she lives with her mother, but she waits for her husband to come and take her home. Esperanza brings her books. One day, Esperanza memorizes and recites "The Walrus and the Carpenter" from *Through the Looking Glass*. The beauty of Esperanza's recital moves Ruthie, but she cannot express herself. Instead, she tells Esperanza she has beautiful teeth.

Summary: "The Earl of Tennessee"
Earl, another of Esperanza's neighbors, is a jukebox repairman who works nights and is seen only when he comes out to tell the children sitting in front of his door to keep quiet. He has two lively dogs, and occasionally he gives the children old jukebox records. Earl supposedly has a wife, and many of the neighbors claim to have seen her, but everyone describes her differently. Earl clearly has a series of women whom he brings to his apartment for quick visits every now and then.

Summary: "Sire"
Sire is Esperanza's first real crush. He is a neighborhood boy who sometimes stares at her. Esperanza always tries to stare straight ahead when she passes him and not to be afraid. Her parents tell her Sire is a punk and that she shouldn't talk to him. Sire has a pretty, petite girlfriend, Lois, who doesn't know how to tie her shoes. Esperanza watches Sire and Lois take walks, or Lois riding Sire's bike. Esperanza wonders what it would be like to be in Lois's place, but her parents say that Lois is the kind of girl who goes into alleys. That doesn't keep Esperanza from wishing she could sit up outside late at night on the steps with Sire, or from wondering what it feels like to be held by a boy, something she so far has felt only in her dreams.

Summary: "Four Skinny Trees"
Esperanza compares herself to the trees outside her house. She thinks that both she and the trees do not belong in the barrio, but are stuck there anyway. Both she and they have secret strength and anger. The trees teach her not to forget her reason for being. They

inspire her because they have grown despite the concrete that tries to keep them in the ground.

ANALYSIS
Ruthie demonstrates the limited nature of a child's perspective, but her section also brings up the darker, very adult subject of death. Despite Ruthie's childishness, Esperanza hopes she'll act as another Aunt Lupe and encourage her to create art, but Ruthie is either not mature or not aware enough to be of any help. Whether she is mentally handicapped or mentally ill is not clear, and whether her statements about her past are true is also a mystery. Although Ruthie shares some of Esperanza's poetic talents, Esperanza can see more of people's motives than Ruthie can, which makes her more adult than Ruthie. Because of Ruthie's many limitations, she is another figure who, like Geraldo in the last section, represents the ultimate outcast—she fits into neither the child's world nor the world of adults. Angel Vargas, the boy who fell and died in "There Was an Old Woman She Had So Many Children She Didn't Know What to Do," reappears in this section, which indicates that Esperanza met Ruthie fairly early on. However, not until she needs someone else to listen to her read poetry does Esperanza feel compelled to mention Ruthie. Angel Vargas's reappearance in this section acts as a reminder that death lurks everywhere and that it doesn't affect only older people, such as those who died in the previous sections.

The womanizing Earl reveals the neighborhood's vastly different standards for men and women regarding sex. Earl is one of the few grown men actually present in the barrio during the day. While Ruthie innocently waits for her husband to return for her, neighbors gossip about a wife Earl abandoned. He brings home many women, and different people believe different women might be his wife, though these women are most likely prostitutes. Esperanza notes off-handedly that no one in the neighborhood can agree on what Earl's wife actually looks like. This is one of Esperanza's more naïve observations, since the adults in the neighborhood are almost certainly aware that these "wives" are all different women. Associating sex with marriage and love is a child's mistake, but the neighbors, who insist, seriously or otherwise, that all these different women are somehow his one "wife," perpetuate the misunderstanding. No ugly judgments are made about Earl. He can do as he pleases with as many women as he wants, while Lois from "Sire" already has a bad reputation as a sexually willing and available girl.

Esperanza dreams of being Sire's girlfriend, and this fantasy suggests one possible and dangerous path Esperanza may take through adolescence. She desires to be in Lois's place, even though Lois, Sire's girlfriend, is passive and helpless. When Esperanza says that Lois cannot tie her own shoes but Esperanza herself can, she naïvely believes that Sire might like her better than Lois because of her competence. However, on some level Esperanza realizes that Lois's attractiveness actually lies in her incompetence. One of the reasons Esperanza does not have a boyfriend like Sire is that her parents strongly discourage it, telling her not to talk to punks like Sire. However, Esperanza may not need her parents' advice in order to decide not to be like Lois. Her dreams and thoughts about Sire are rooted in an idealistic view of sex. In her dreams she can control the narrative, whereas in reality her constant need to be "brave" in front of Sire signifies the threat to her selfhood that sex represents. Even more threatening, Esperanza is nowhere near as helpless as Lois, and her talents and intelligence complicate the neighborhood's acceptable image of attractiveness and femininity. Esperanza's observation that Lois's helplessness made her attractive to Sire suggests her insecurities about her own ability to attract men.

In "The Earl of Tennessee" and "Four Skinny Trees," Esperanza's language indicates that she is beginning to find beauty in the everyday ugliness that surrounds her. In the first section, Esperanza complains that her house has no front yard, only four little elms in front of it. However, in "Four Skinny Trees," Esperanza finds inspiration and beauty in these skinny, jagged trees, qualities she couldn't see when she first moved to Mango Street. Esperanza shows growth as a writer when she is able to empathize with a man, her father, in "Papa Who Wakes Up Tired in the Dark." Now, she shows that she has moved to another level of empathy and observation by being able to identify with inanimate objects. In "The Earl of Tennessee," Esperanza says that Earl's dogs "leap and somersault like an apostrophe and comma." Here again, Esperanza shows mature writerly instincts. She sees vitality in these punctuation marks, which other kids most likely view as boring grammar.

SECTIONS 30–33

SUMMARY: "NO SPEAK ENGLISH"

Mamacita is the wife of one of Esperanza's neighbors. Her husband works very hard to bring her and her child to Mango Street, but once Mamacita arrives, she never leaves the house. She misses Mexico and refuses to assimilate. She is hugely fat, but Esperanza also finds her beautiful. She sits by the window, listens to Spanish radio, and wishes to go home. Some people think she never leaves her room because she is too fat or because she cannot get down the three flights of stairs, but Esperanza believes she refuses to come down because she doesn't speak any English. Esperanza's father explains how hard it is to live in the United States without knowing English, saying that when he first arrived, the only food he knew was "hamandeggs," so he had to eat hamandeggs three times a day. The final blow for Mamacita is that her child, whom she has brought with her from Mexico, learns English. It breaks her heart that even he insists upon speaking this ugly language that she cannot understand.

SUMMARY: "RAFAELA WHO DRINKS COCONUT & PAPAYA JUICE ON TUESDAYS"

On Tuesdays, when Rafaela's husband has his poker game, he locks her in their third-floor apartment because she is so beautiful, he's afraid she'll escape. She spends these afternoons and evenings leaning out the window, which makes her prematurely old. She wants to go dance at the bar down the street while she is still young, but instead she has to drop a dollar out of the window so that Esperanza and her friends can buy her some coconut or papaya juice at the store, which Rafaela then hauls up on a clothesline. At the bar, women who are older than Rafaela are allowed to dance and flirt, but each risks being imprisoned in the same way as Rafaela.

SUMMARY: "SALLY"

Sally is extremely beautiful. She wears Cleopatra makeup, nylons, and short skirts. At school she leans against the fence, and all the boys spread vicious gossip about her. Sally's father thinks her beauty is dangerous and doesn't let her out of the house, but Esperanza thinks Sally is wonderful and would like to be her new best friend. She wants to learn to line her eyes as Sally does. Esperanza understands that Sally wishes she didn't have to go home after school so she wouldn't have to worry about her father, gossip, or not belonging.

SUMMARY: "MINERVA WRITES POEMS"

Minerva is only two years older than Esperanza, but she is married with two children. Her husband has left her, but he sometimes returns, only to leave again. At night, after the children go to bed and she is alone, Minerva writes poems. She shares her poems with Esperanza, and Esperanza shares hers. However, Minerva also continues to take her husband back, even when he beats her. She visits Esperanza one night after being beaten up and asks for advice, but Esperanza cannot offer any. She doesn't know what will happen to Minerva.

ANALYSIS

Each of the four women in these sections represents a possible fate for women on Mango Street, and they appear in the order of how similar they are to Esperanza, as well as in the order of how vulnerable they are. Such ordering suggests the urgency of Esperanza's situation. Mamacita is from Mexico and is stuck because of language, which is one thing Esperanza will not have to worry about. Rafaela has become prematurely old, which distances her from Esperanza. While Sally is Esperanza's age, she is not as similar to Esperanza as is poetic Minerva. Minerva and Esperanza are nearly the same age and are both aspiring poets. Although Mamacita is unhappy, her sadness springs from her own helplessness, not from her husband. Rafaela is trapped at home, but she does have the freedom to make exchanges with the children through the window. Sally is completely under her father's thumb, and Minerva is in constant personal danger. While other women can sit by the window to dream, Minerva's husband throws a rock through her window. When Minerva comes to Esperanza for guidance, Esperanza says she can do nothing to help. Esperanza will have to work hard, and quickly, if she does not want to end up like Minerva.

In "No Speak English," Esperanza sees that not knowing the language can keep people caged. Without language, Mamacita is miserable. While others make fun of her appearance, Esperanza views Mamacita as a tragic figure. She believes Mamacita is stuck at home because of the language barrier. In other vignettes, Esperanza has associated naming and linguistic ability with power and freedom, and here, she shows that the converse of that theory is true. Because Mamacita does not speak English, she must live her life in a cage. In Esperanza's experience, language leads to freedom. If self-expression does equal freedom as Esperanza hypothesizes, becoming a writer suddenly makes sense as the perfect way to escape the neighborhood.

SECTIONS 34–36

SUMMARY: "BUMS IN THE ATTIC"

Esperanza wants a nice suburban house with a garden, like the ones where her father works. On the weekends, the family visits these houses and dreams about moving there. Esperanza has stopped going with her family. She, too, would like to live in one of those houses, but she is tired of looking at what she cannot have. She imagines that when she owns one of these houses in the future, she will not forget where she is from. When bums pass her house she will invite them in and give them a place to live in her attic, because she knows, she says, "how it is to be without a house." When people think that the squeaking in the attic is rats, she will shake her head and say it is bums.

SUMMARY: "BEAUTIFUL & CRUEL"

Esperanza worries that she is unattractive and that her looks will leave her stuck at home. Her sister, who is more attractive, wants a husband to take her away, but she doesn't want to leave by having a baby with just any man, as Minerva's sister did. Esperanza's mother comforts Esperanza by saying she will be more beautiful as she gets older, but Esperanza has decided not to wait around for a husband to take her away. Instead, she wants to be like the femme fatales in movies who drive the men crazy and then refuse them. These women do not give their power away. Esperanza's way of beginning to be like this is to leave the dinner table like a man, without pushing in her chair or doing her dishes.

SUMMARY: "A SMART COOKIE"

Esperanza's mother complains that she could have done something with her life. She has many skills—she can speak two languages, sing, draw, and fix a television—but she does not know how to use the subway. While making a family meal, Esperanza's mother sings along to a *Madame Butterfly* record she has borrowed from the public library. She tells Esperanza that she needs to be able to take care of herself and not just rely on a man. She gives as examples two of her friends, one whose husband has left and the other who is a widow. Then she describes how when she was younger she dropped out of school, not because she lacked intelligence, but because she was ashamed about not having nice clothes. She seems disgusted with her young self and tells Esperanza not to be like she was.

ANALYSIS

Esperanza finally matures and realizes that she needs to change her strategy in trying to get what she wants. She separates herself from her family, refusing to go with them to visit houses in the suburbs because she no longer wants to dream about a house. Rather, she wants to go and get one. She resolves not to forget her origins. Until this point, Esperanza has expressed nothing but a desire to leave her neighborhood, never to return. Now she dreams of letting homeless bums from the neighborhood live with her in her imaginary home away from Mango Street. She has begun to understand that her perfect suburbs on the hill are flawed because they have no system for including people like her. Esperanza suspects that if she escapes the barrio, she will not be satisfied by a suburban world that ignores the existence of less privileged people.

Esperanza decides how she'll approach her future in "Bums in the Attic," while in "Beautiful & Cruel," she decides how she will define herself sexually. Her new thoughts, however, introduce new problems. Tragic women like Minerva and Rafaela in the previous sections have reaffirmed Esperanza's desire to be independent. As a femme fatale, Esperanza can be independent without ignoring her new sexual awareness. She understands that adult sexuality is tied up with independence, and that to accept men is to give up her autonomy. She also decides she will not spend her time doing petty tasks like washing the dishes, tasks she could spend time doing every day without ever really accomplishing anything. However, Esperanza's solution presents a problem. By standing up and leaving her dishes on the table, she is creating more work for another woman. Yet there is no room in Esperanza's imagination to make society fairer by asking that men and women share tedious tasks like doing the dishes.

In the opinion of Esperanza's mother, to be a "smart cookie" is not a positive attribute. She gives the example of dropping out of school because her clothes were not nice as an example of being a "smart cookie." If you think you are too smart for school or too smart to take your mother's advice, her mother is saying, then you'll end up with a husband when you're too young and will have no way to escape. Esperanza has to realize that she is not smarter than the women around her. Surrounded by clever and creative women, Esperanza can view none of them, including her own mother, as role models because they are stuck on Mango Street. Her mother knows how to do everything except take the subway—that is, she knows how to do everything but leave. Esperanza finds her mother's frankness about her regrets surprising, which suggests that their relationship is not usually so open and honest. Her mother compares her friends to Madame Butterfly, a character in an opera who spends her life waiting for her lover to return. This observation plays on Esperanza's earlier thesis that the Chinese and the Mexicans do not like their women strong.

Sections 37–40

Sally, you lied, you lied. He wouldn't let me go. He said I love you, I love you, Spanish girl.

(*See* Quotations, *p. 52*)

Summary: "What Sally Said"

Sally's father beats her. She comes to school bruised and says she fell, but it's easy to see she's been beaten. She tells Esperanza that one time her father beat her with his hands instead of with a belt. Sally's father is afraid she'll run off with a man and bring shame to the family like his sisters did. At one point Sally asks to come and stay with Esperanza's family. She brings over a bag and prepares to move in, but that evening her father comes by with tears in his eyes. He apologizes and asks her to come home. She does, and she is safe for a while. However, one day Sally's father sees Sally talking to a boy. He beats her with a belt and then with his fists. She is injured so badly that she misses two days of school.

Summary: "The Monkey Garden"

A family with a pet monkey moves away, and the neighborhood kids take over the garden behind their house. The garden quickly becomes a dump for old cars and other trash, but to the children it is a magical place where anything is possible. They explore it, looking for the old, lost things the garden keeps. One day Esperanza is there with Sally. Esperanza wants to run around with the boys, but Sally stays to the side. She does not like to get her stockings dirty, and she plays a more grown-up game by talking to the boys. Tito, a neighborhood boy, steals Sally's keys, and he and his friends tell her that she has to kiss all of them to get them back. Sally agrees, and they go behind an old car. Esperanza wants to save Sally from being exploited this way, so she runs to tell Tito's mother what the boys are doing. His mother doesn't care, and Esperanza sets out to save Sally herself. Arming herself with a brick, she confronts the boys.

Sally and the boys laugh at her and tell her to go away. Esperanza hides beneath a tree and tries to will her heart to stop. When she finally gets up she looks at her feet, which look clunky and unfamiliar. The garden seems unfamiliar too.

SUMMARY: "RED CLOWNS"

Esperanza narrates this section after she has been sexually assaulted by a group of boys, and though she gives her impressions and expresses her confusion, she never specifies exactly what the boys do to her. We know Esperanza goes to a carnival with Sally and that she enjoys watching Sally on the rides. Sally seems careless and free, and at one point she disappears with an older boy. While Esperanza waits for Sally to return, a group of non-Latino boys attacks Esperanza. The event is nothing like sexual encounters Esperanza has seen in the movies or read in magazines, or even like what Sally has told her. She is traumatized and keeps hearing the voice of one of the boys saying mockingly, "I love you, Spanish girl." She blames Sally for abandoning her and not being there to save her, and her anger spreads to all the women who have not told her what sex is really like.

SUMMARY: "LINOLEUM ROSES"

Sally marries before the end of the year. She marries a much older salesman who has to take her to another state where it is legal to marry girls who are under fourteen. Esperanza believes Sally married to escape her house. Sally claims to be happy because her husband sometimes gives her money, but her husband sometimes becomes violent and angry as well. He does not let her go out, talk on the phone, see her friends, or even look out the window. Sally spends her days sitting at home and looking at the domestic objects around her.

ANALYSIS

Esperanza's love for her friend Sally translates into a violent need to protect Sally from the outside world, and in this way Esperanza resembles Sally's father and Sally's husband. Esperanza wants to keep the boys away from Sally, just as the men do. However, unlike them, Esperanza saves her violence for the boys. In "The Monkey Garden," she threatens the boys with sticks and a brick. For Esperanza, Sally is part of a possible new lifestyle that she tries on for a little while, abandoning her former friends for her stylish, beautiful, and sexy new one. While Esperanza interprets Sally's sexual experience as maturity when she first meets her, she eventually discovers that Sally's search for sexual experiences is actually a desperate attempt to escape her violent father. Sally's father is one of the worst characters in *The House on Mango Street*, but when Sally manages to escape him, she finds someone equally bad. She gives up her education to live with a man who does not even let her look out the window. Looking out the window is the last bit of freedom for most of the trapped women Esperanza knows, including Mamacita, Marin, and Rafaela, but Sally is not even allowed to do that. Esperanza tried to protect Sally, but Sally is fated now to a life of looking at the artificial roses on her linoleum floor.

The monkey garden, much like the Garden of Eden, is the place where Esperanza loses a large measure of her innocence, and when Esperanza loses her innocent ideals about her friends and community, she cannot return to the garden. For Esperanza and other young people, the monkey garden is a place of childhood games, but Sally and the boys use it for a more grown-up purpose by hiding behind a car and experimenting sexually. Esperanza is appalled by the complicity of the women in her neighborhood with what she sees as the boys' sexual manipulation of Sally. The boys are playing a game with Sally that only they can win. Tito's mother doesn't seem to care, and her indifference gives the boys tacit permission for what they are doing. Additionally, Sally does not want to be saved. Esperanza is dismayed to see that Sally, too, approves of the boys' manipulation. Esperanza is ashamed that she put herself at such personal risk, arming herself with a brick, only to be laughed away by the girl she tried to protect. The garden has become a place of danger and confusion, and it is no longer hers.

When a group of anonymous boys assaults Esperanza, she directs her anger toward women and society instead of toward the specific boys responsible. She rages at Sally for not being there and not telling her what sex is really like, and at society for not debunking the myth that sex is connected with love and romance. Sally has proven to be an unreliable friend, always choosing boys' attention over Esperanza's friendship, and Esperanza now pays the price for her loyalty. Esperanza's lack of explicit anger toward her attackers suggests that in Esperanza's world, any man or boy could have been guilty, but women are the ones responsible for keeping each other safe. In "Red Clowns," Esperanza's voice takes on uncharacteristic childish innocence. Esperanza has matured a great deal over the course of a year, but this violent experience renders her helpless and scared. She blames what she knows. Blaming her attackers would require a well of strength she has not yet developed.

SECTIONS 41–44

No, this isn't my house I say and shake my head as if
shaking could undo the year I've lived here. I don't
belong. I don't ever want to come from here.
(See QUOTATIONS, *p. 53)*

SUMMARY: "THE THREE SISTERS"

Lucy and Rachel's baby sister dies. The neighborhood gathers in Lucy and Rachel's house to view the baby before she is buried. Three of the guests are old aunts. Esperanza finds them fascinating and thinks they are magical. The sisters can tell that Esperanza is uncomfortable at the wake and call her over to talk to her. They compliment Esperanza on her name and tell her she is special and that she will go far. They tell her to make a wish, so Esperanza does, and then they tell her it will come true. One of the women takes Esperanza aside and tells her that even though she will be able to leave, she should come back for the others. She has guessed Esperanza's wish, and Esperanza feels guilty for wishing for such a selfish thing. The woman tells her she will always be Mango Street.

SUMMARY: "ALICIA & I TALKING ON EDNA'S STEPS"

Esperanza is jealous of Alicia because she has a town to call home, Guadalajara, and she will return there someday. Alicia observes that Esperanza already has a home. But Esperanza shakes her head. She does not want to have lived in the house for a year, or to come from Mango Street. She declares that she will never come back to Mango Street until someone makes it better. Then Alicia asks who will make it better, suggesting the mayor as a possibility. The girls laugh because the idea of the mayor coming to Mango Street is so far outside the realm of possibility.

SUMMARY: "A HOUSE OF MY OWN"

Esperanza describes the qualities and parts of her ideal house: picturesque, not belonging to a man, flowers in front, a porch, and her shoes beside the bed. She describes the house as safe and full of potential, "clean as paper before the poem."

SUMMARY: "MANGO SAYS GOODBYE SOMETIMES"

Esperanza defines herself as a storyteller. She frames the story by saying she is going to tell the audience a story about a girl who did not want to belong. She repeats the paragraph from the first chapter about having not always lived on Mango Street, naming the other streets she has lived on. The house on Mango Street is the one she remembers the most. When she writes about it, she is able to free herself from the house's grip. She knows that one day she will pack her books and writing materials and leave Mango Street, but she will have left only to come back for the others who cannot get out on their own.

ANALYSIS

The old women's palm reading at the wake differs significantly from Esperanza's earlier visit to the fortuneteller Elenita. This time, fate seems to have sought out Esperanza: The sisters call to her, whereas earlier Esperanza pursued Elenita. Though Esperanza doubted Elenita's prediction, she is now more willing to believe in an external source of wisdom that may not have a logical explanation. More important, while Elenita used Tarot cards to predict Esperanza's future, the sisters read the future in Esperanza's own hand, which seems to make the prediction more personal. Esperanza has not yet left Mango Street physically, but she is already gone spiritually, and the sisters sense this. They encourage her to be faithful to the experiences that have shaped her and sympathetic to those who lack her abilities and her will to escape. They want her to accept herself for who she is, including her name. The three women resemble the three Fates from Greek mythology, who spin a string for each human's life. One spins the thread and controls birth, the second measures and spins the events of the human life, and the third decides the moment of death and cuts the thread. Like the mythological Fates, these three women seem to know Esperanza's destiny just by looking at her. The women's relationship to these mythical figures gives their advice to Esperanza more weight.

Although she does not say so, Esperanza, like Alicia, realizes that if Mango Street is ever to improve, it will have to be through the efforts of people like her who escape, become successful, and then return. Esperanza spends time with Alicia at the end of *The House on Mango Street*, instead of with Sally, who has married and dropped out of middle school. Alicia is pursuing her own form of escape by working hard to attend college, and she has not married. Although Alicia has a difficult family situation, she has not turned her back on her roots. Instead, she is doing what she can, the hard way, to make an eventual change. Alicia provides the final step in Esperanza's escape from Mango Street: she instills in her a sense of responsibility to who she is. Rather than trying to be someone else or to escape through someone else, as Sally did, Esperanza needs to work with what she has and eventually come to terms with her roots. Even if she leaves it, Mango Street can be incorporated into her future home.

As *The House on Mango Street* draws to a close, we see that little tangible change has taken place in Esperanza's life, although she has matured physically and emotionally. After her traumatic experiences as Sally's friend, Esperanza returns to her original, less dangerous best friends, Lucy and Rachel. She has spent a year in the neighborhood, and no physical signs suggest that she is anywhere near actually leaving. However, the emotional groundwork for her escape is in place, and she has already found one method of escaping: writing. Writing has proven therapeutic, even lifesaving, for Esperanza. It is her "home in the heart," which suggests that Elenita's reading of the Tarot cards was accurate after all. The same sensitivities that made Esperanza so vulnerable to being hurt by the hardships of life on Mango Street have also enabled her to escape it spiritually through writing. Although she will live in the neighborhood for a few more years, she has reconciled herself to it. She will write her own narrative of life on Mango Street, and when she does leave the neighborhood, she will write somewhere else.

The last two sections of *The House on Mango Street*, "A House of My Own" and "Mango Says Goodbye Sometimes," exhibit language that, though less mature than many other sections, is highly poetic. The first paragraph of "Mango Says Goodbye Sometimes" consists of repetitive, Dr. Seuss-style rhymes and rhythms. Esperanza's thirteen-year-old written voice comes through here. She has been narrating the story all along, but now she is writing it. This shift explains why the voice seems to be less mature in these final sections—this voice is actually Esperanza's young but burgeoning written voice. Esperanza's story is about a girl who did not want to belong. By writing this, Esperanza has made an important realization: she *does* belong on Mango Street. Both Alicia and the sisters help Esperanza come to this conclusion. Esperanza is not on Mango Street by mistake, as she would like to believe, but because she belongs there, at least for now.

Important Quotations Explained

1. In English my name means hope. In Spanish it means too
   many letters. It means sadness, it means waiting.

This quotation, from the section "My Name," occurs before Esperanza says her name for the first time. Esperanza's characterization of her name shows how she channels her dissatisfaction with her given name into creativity and word play. What Esperanza says here about the word *esperanza* is neither intuitive nor true. In Spanish, *esperanza* means "hope." The word does not have a dictionary definition in English. When Esperanza says her name means "waiting," she has taken the Spanish verb *esperar*, which means "to wait or expect," and superimposed it on the noun *hope*. Similarly, sadness may come from the opposite of *esperanza*, *desesperarse*, or "despair." Later in the chapter Esperanza says she would like to give herself a new name, but she has already given her old name new meaning, using a similar-looking word with a different definition. By refusing to accept the word's conventional definitions, Esperanza shows that she possesses a writer's gift for interpretation and storytelling.

On a more literal level, the words Esperanza has chosen to associate with the Spanish meaning of her name are very negative. She has taken a positive word, *hope*, and given it three negative descriptions. The first, "too many letters," is a description of the word as it is written. As an American schoolgirl, Esperanza is frustrated by the physical difficulty of her name, which sets her apart from others. Even her siblings, Nenny, Carlos, and Kiki, have simpler, less foreign-sounding names. The next two negative descriptions are associations she has with herself. As her current self with her current name, Esperanza's life is full of sadness and waiting. Esperanza says her inner self is described by the name "Zeze the X." Zeze the X is the version of Esperanza who does not belong in the barrio.

2.　　Until then I am a red balloon, a balloon tied to an anchor.

Esperanza describes herself as a red balloon in "Boys and Girls" before she has made any friends in her new neighborhood. Until she has a best friend with whom she can share her secrets and who will understand her jokes, she believes she will be this red balloon. The image of the balloon suggests that she feels she is floating in anticipation of something and that she feels isolated. The color red suggests that she stands out in the neighborhood. Esperanza finds friends, Lucy and Rachel, soon after this section, but the feeling of being a balloon persists. She is still floating because she feels she does not fit in on Mango Street, and she is still isolated because she does not share her deepest secrets with her friends. In "Laughter" we learn that Esperanza's sister Nenny, not her new friends, laughs at her jokes without her having to explain them.

Esperanza has chosen to think of herself as something floating, and in this way she is similar to some of the other children on Mango Street. Both Meme Ortiz and Angel Vargas fall from great heights in early vignettes. Meme breaks both his arms, while Angel dies. Both children are trying to fly in order to escape their lives on Mango Street. In this quote Esperanza describes herself as floating, but also as tethered to the earth. When she finally abandons her tether, she would like to fly away instead of falling, as the others have. She will either have to find a way to return to the ground without hurting herself, or to fly away without falling. By the end of *The House on Mango Street*, Esperanza discovers she is not unique in her neighborhood, but does, in fact, belong there. Only at that point can Esperanza let go of this particular metaphor and realize that she cannot float away from her community for good. She must leave it gradually and eventually return.

QUOTATIONS

3. She looked out the window her whole life, the way so many women sit their sadness on an elbow. I wonder if she made the best with what she got or was she sorry because she couldn't be all the things she wanted to be. Esperanza. I have inherited her name, but I don't want to inherit her place by the window.

Esperanza says this of her great-grandmother and namesake, Esperanza. Her great-grandmother is the first of many women in *The House on Mango Street* who spend their lives looking out the window and longing for escape. Esperanza resolves not to end up like her great-grandmother even before she meets the other trapped women on Mango Street. These modern women, including Mamacita, Rafaela, Minerva (whose window is broken), and Sally (who has to look at the floor instead of out the window) give Esperanza an even more vivid picture of what it is like to be trapped, hardening her resolve not to be like the first Esperanza.

By repeatedly connecting the window image to the trapped women on Mango Street, Cisneros depicts a row of third-floor apartments as jail cells. Some of the women are stuck in these cells because of their husbands, but Esperanza implies that some of them could do more to change their situations. Esperanza wonders if her great-grandmother made the best of her situation, or if instead she turned her anger at her husband inward, and therefore hurt herself more than her husband could have. Esperanza asks this question only once, and she does not apply it to any of the other women she meets. Her capacity for both empathy and pity grows as she understands their particular stories better than the story of her great-grandmother, whom she never met.

4.   Sally, you lied, you lied. He wouldn't let me go. He said I
      love you, I love you, Spanish girl.

Esperanza says this in "Red Clowns," after a group of boys has sexually assaulted her at a carnival. She repeats the accusation that her
friend lied, blaming Sally for the assault instead of the boys who
have hurt and traumatized her. Esperanza blames Sally for not
returning after she goes off with an older boy, but the accusation
goes deeper than that. Esperanza is angry that girls perpetuate the
myth that sex goes hand in hand with love. "I love you, Spanish
girl" is a taunting, violent refrain that has no place in the picture of
sex that popular culture presents to young girls. Esperanza understands that popular media may never change, but at the very least
the women who have more experience, like Sally, should debunk the
myth so reality would not be such a surprise to girls like Esperanza.

    Esperanza's accusation here is the culmination of a theme that is
implicit in much of *The House on Mango Street*: men will not
change, so women need to help each other. In "The Monkey Garden," the section before "Red Clowns," Esperanza sees Tito's
mother as complicit in Sally's exploitation, since she refuses to see
that her son is doing something wrong. Esperanza reacts by crying
alone in a corner of the Monkey Garden. In "Red Clowns," Esperanza's pain is more acute. She screams out her accusation. Her experience with the disloyal Sally leads to Esperanza's resolution to come
back to help the other women on Mango Street once she leaves. She
does not want to leave the women behind in a dangerous place the
way Sally left her.

5.   No, this isn't my house I say and shake my head as if shaking
     could undo the year I've lived here. I don't belong. I don't
     ever want to come from here.

This is Esperanza's reply to Alicia in "Alicia & I Talking on Edna's
Steps" after Alicia insists that Esperanza does have a house, and that
it is right there on Mango Street. This exchange occurs near the end
of the novel, when Esperanza is realizing she does indeed belong on
Mango Street. Instead of insisting that she does not belong, here she
says she doesn't *want* to belong, which suggests that Esperanza
understands that she actually does. She has realized that she is not
intrinsically different from the other women in her neighborhood.
She has met other women in the neighborhood who write, women
who share her desire to escape, women who are interested in boys,
and women, like Alicia, who desire education. Her previous feelings
of superiority and difference were only childish ways of obscuring
the truth: Mango Street is part of Esperanza. No matter how far she
goes, she will never truly escape it.

QUOTATIONS

KEY FACTS

FULL TITLE
The House on Mango Street

AUTHOR
Sandra Cisneros

TYPE OF WORK
Novel made up of interconnected vignettes

GENRE
Coming-of-age story

LANGUAGE
English

TIME AND PLACE WRITTEN
Early 1980s, United States

DATE OF FIRST PUBLICATION
1984

PUBLISHER
Vintage Books (first published by Arte Público Press)

NARRATOR
Esperanza Cordero

POINT OF VIEW
Esperanza narrates in the first-person present tense. She focuses on her day-to-day activities but sometimes narrates sections that are just a series of observations. In later vignettes Esperanza talks less about herself and more about the people around her. In these sections she is never fully omniscient, but she sometimes stretches her imagination to speculate on the characters' feelings and futures.

TONE
Earnest, hopeful, intimate, with very little distance between the implied author and the narrator

TENSE

Mostly present tense, with intermittent incidents told in the future and past tenses

SETTING (TIME)

A period of one year

SETTING (PLACE)

A poor Latino neighborhood in Chicago

PROTAGONIST

Esperanza

MAJOR CONFLICT

Esperanza struggles to find her place in her neighborhood and in the world.

RISING ACTION

Esperanza desires to leave her neighborhood, observes other women, and finds newfound sexual awareness in her friendship with the sexually adventurous Sally.

CLIMAX

Esperanza's tumultuous friendship with Sally leads to her emotional and sexual humiliation.

FALLING ACTION

Esperanza returns to her less mature friends, understands that she does in fact belong on Mango Street, and settles on writing as her way of both escaping and accepting her neighborhood.

THEMES

The power of language; the struggle for self-definition; sexuality vs. autonomy; women's unfulfilled responsibilities to each other

MOTIFS

Names; falling; women by windows

SYMBOLS

Shoes; trees; poetry

FORESHADOWING

The bum's request for a kiss; the boys' demand that Sally kiss each of them in exchange for her keys; the description of Esperanza's great-grandmother's life of sitting at the window; Esperanza's preoccupation with names and naming.

KEY FACTS

Study Questions and Essay Topics

Study Questions

1. What role does death play in The House on Mango Street? *How do the many deaths in the novel relate to one another, and how do they influence Esperanza?*

Five people die in *The House on Mango Street*: Angel Vargas, Esperanza's grandfather, Aunt Lupe, Geraldo, and Rachel and Lucy's baby sister. Spanning all ages, these characters include an infant, a boy, a young man in his twenties, and two elderly figures. The deaths of the young people show that Mango Street is a dangerous place to grow up. Geraldo dies because of a bad hospital's neglect, and Angel's death is due to negligent parenting. These deaths are a reminder that these children's lives are fragile, and that although Esperanza describes her neighborhood as normal, it is not actually a safe environment for children. These deaths also play an important role in pushing Esperanza toward finding her place in the adult world.

Angel Vargas is the first character to die in *The House on Mango Street*, and Esperanza does not take his death to heart. She compares him to a falling doughnut: it is a death that causes no noise from him or from the community, and it has no emotional resonance for her. When her grandfather dies, however, Esperanza must look at death more seriously. Angel's death does not lead Esperanza to imagine what it would be like if one of *her* siblings were to die, but when her grandfather dies, she tries to put herself in her father's shoes and imagine how she would feel if he died. When Esperanza's Aunt Lupe dies in the following chapter, Esperanza does not need to feel empathy. She feels both sad and responsible for her aunt's death. This escalation of feeling suggests that Esperanza is maturing emotionally. By the end of the novel, Esperanza is still working on the process of coming to terms with death. She attends Rachel and Lucy's sister's wake and feels uncomfortable and out of place. However, she is beginning to perceive death as something with real consequences. The three sisters Esperanza meets at the wake encourage her to help the living by remembering the other women in her community.

THE HOUSE ON MANGO STREET ❧ 57

2.   *What role does magic or the supernatural play in* THE
      HOUSE ON MANGO STREET? *How does it affect and
      influence Esperanza?*

Esperanza encounters women she associates with magical powers
twice in the novel. The first time, she seeks out Elenita, a witch
woman, who gives her an unsatisfactory Tarot card reading. The
second time, three sisters Esperanza describes as not related to "anything but the moon" speak to her at a wake. In both cases, the
women speak truth in their own way. Elenita tells Esperanza she will
have a house in the heart, and eventually Esperanza finds exactly
that, through the solace writing gives her. The sisters tell Esperanza
that her wish for a house away from Mango Street will come true.
While Esperanza never actually leaves Mango Street, her assured voice
in the last chapter suggests she will do so eventually, and that when she
does, she will heed the sisters' advice and return to help others.

Even though these women are prescient in some ways, it is difficult for Esperanza to believe or understand them. When she is with
Elenita, Esperanza lies about her hand feeling cold. Elenita's apartment seems more normal than spiritual to Esperanza, since she
hears a Bugs Bunny cartoon and a crying baby in the background.
She is disappointed by Elenita's prophecy. Esperanza is more willing
to believe the sisters' prophecy because they predict that Esperanza
will get what she wants. However, she is confused by their advice to
return to the neighborhood. Esperanza does not see the supernatural in
her Aunt Lupe, but her aunt's advice, that writing will set her free, is just
as perceptive as the advice she receives from Elenita and the sisters.
What Esperanza sees as magic may actually be just sound advice.

3. *Discuss the role of parents in the novel. How can Esperanza's relationship with her parents be characterized? In what ways is it different or similar to other characters' parent/child relationships in the novel?*

Esperanza defines herself as being completely separate from her parents. For most of *The House on Mango Street*, she clings to the belief that she does not belong in her house or in her neighborhood. She distances herself from her house physically by spending most of her time outdoors, and she distances herself from it emotionally by denying her place there. In both cases, Esperanza is distancing herself from her parents. Finding an independent existence away from them is an important part of growing up, and throughout the novel, Esperanza searches for new role models among the women in her neighborhood. She further distances herself from her parents by refusing to go on their weekend visits to the suburbs to dream about houses. In doing so, she gives up a rare opportunity to spend time with her family—particularly her hard-working father—because she is tired of seeing nice houses that she cannot have.

Despite Esperanza's efforts to be independent of her parents, they do play a crucial role in her life. All around Esperanza are examples of bad parents: Sally's father beats her, Minerva's father left her mother, Minerva's husband leaves his children, and the Vargas kids' father has abandoned them. Similarly, Ruthie's mother Edna shows no love for her daughter, and Tito's mother does not care how Tito behaves toward girls. Esperanza's parents at least set a good example and try to instill values in their daughter. They advise Esperanza not to hang around with Sire, a neighborhood punk, and Esperanza's mother tells her never to be ashamed as she was in her youth. Her parents show that they value education highly by sending their children to a private Catholic school they can barely afford. Esperanza may not like where her parents have chosen to live, but at least their home is not dangerous, which might force Esperanza into early marriage as a way of escape. Though Esperanza may not acknowledge or appreciate them, her parents are significant role models.

Suggested Essay Topics

1. *What is the purpose of the internal rhymes that appear in many vignettes? Provide a detailed reading of a section's rhyming words, explaining how the rhymes contribute to the meaning of that section as a whole.*

2. *How do race and gender come into conflict in* The House on Mango Street*? Does one triumph as the more important concern, or do both issues receive equal consideration?*

3. *How are sex and violence linked in this novel? Why does Esperanza both seek and try to avoid sexual experiences?*

4. *In what ways does writing set Esperanza apart from her neighborhood? In what ways does it help her integrate into her neighborhood?*

5. *Why do you think Cisneros chooses not to try to represent dialect, slang, or accents? Is her language ever particularly "Chicano" or "Latino"?*

Review and Resources

Quiz

1. Who makes Esperanza feel ashamed of her previous house by making her point it out while she is playing in the street?

    A.   Cathy
    B.   A marshmallow salesman
    C.   A priest
    D.   A nun

2. Who pushes Esperanza into the water in front of a fire hydrant?

    A.   Kiki and Carlos
    B.   Darius
    C.   Sire
    D.   Tito

3. Who does Esperanza decide to let live in the attic of her dream house?

    A.   Bums
    B.   A cat
    C.   Her little sister, Nenny
    D.   Her friend Minerva

4. When Esperanza talks about clouds and hips with her friends, how does she describe them?

    A.   Metaphorically
    B.   With respect to her everyday life
    C.   Scientifically
    D.   With the names of people on her block

5. What do Esperanza and her friends do to imitate grown-ups?

    A. Put on makeup
    B. Wear high-heeled shoes
    C. Smoke cigarettes
    D. Dye their hair

6. Which one of these women does NOT spend her days sitting by the window?

    A. Esperanza's great-grandmother
    B. Esperanza's mother
    C. Rafaela
    D. Mamacita

7. Who is the first person to whom Esperanza recites one of her poems?

    A. Her mother
    B. Her Aunt Lupe
    C. Ruthie
    D. Lucy, Rachel, and Nenny

8. What is Esperanza's first job?

    A. Working in a store
    B. Helping Marin sell cosmetics
    C. Shelving books at the local library
    D. Sorting negatives at a photofinisher

9. Where is Esperanza's father from?

    A. Mexico
    B. The Dominican Republic
    C. Puerto Rico
    D. Spain

10. What does Esperanza's name mean in Spanish?

    A. "Wisdom"
    B. "Horse"
    C. "Hope"
    D. "Serenity"

REVIEW & RESOURCES

11. Why did Esperanza's mother drop out of school?

    A. She got married

    B. She had a job

    C. She had to move to America

    D. She was ashamed of her clothes

12. What do the three sisters tell Esperanza at the wake?

    A. That she should leave Mango Street as soon as she can

    B. That she must come back for the others after she's left Mango Street

    C. That she will never leave Mango Street

    D. That she has a home in the heart

13. Which of Esperanza's friends also writes poetry?

    A. Alicia

    B. Minerva

    C. Marin

    D. Ruthie

14. Where is Esperanza when a group of boys sexually assaults her?

    A. In the Monkey Garden

    B. At a carnival

    C. On Mango Street

    D. At work

15. Which character does not speak English?

    A. Esperanza's father

    B. Marin

    C. Mamacita

    D. Tito

16. Who is the object of Esperanza's first crush?

    A. Sire

    B. Tito

    C. Darius

    D. Geraldo

17. Why does Cathy agree to be Esperanza's friend only until Tuesday?

    A. She has too many cats
    B. Esperanza decides to buy a bike with Lucy and Rachel
    C. Her family is moving out of the neighborhood
    D. She has to go back to France

18. In what way is Nenny similar to Esperanza?

    A. They have the same hair
    B. They make up similar jump-rope rhymes
    C. They both want to eat at the canteen at school
    D. They have the same sense of humor

19. Which of the following is NOT a reason that hips are useful, according to Esperanza, Rachel, and Lucy?

    A. They are good for dancing
    B. They are useful for propping up a baby while cooking
    C. They attract boys
    D. They differentiate the male skeleton from the female one

20. How does Esperanza decide to defy social conventions at home?

    A. She doesn't do her dishes
    B. She refuses to baby-sit her sister, Nenny
    C. She refuses to pick up garbage
    D. She goes out with Sire against her parents' wishes

21. With what object or objects in the neighborhood does Esperanza identify most closely?

    A. Her house
    B. The huge tree in Meme Ortiz's backyard
    C. The four trees in her front yard
    D. The abandoned car in the Monkey Garden

22. What does Nenny want to buy in Gil's junk shop?

    A. A music box
    B. A little Statue of Liberty
    C. A refrigerator
    D. High-heeled shoes

23. What does Esperanza yearn for above all else?

    A. A new name
    B. A home of her own
    C. To become a famous writer
    D. To leave Mango Street

24. Which of Esperanza's friends attends college?

    A. Minerva
    B. Alicia
    C. Sally
    D. Cathy

25. Why doesn't Esperanza want to dance at her cousin's baptismal party?

    A. She doesn't have hips
    B. She thinks her dress is ugly
    C. Nobody asks her to dance
    D. She is wearing her old school shoes

SUGGESTIONS FOR FURTHER READING

BINDER, WOLFGANG, ed. *Partial Autobiographies: Interviews with Twenty Chicano Poets*. Erlangen, Germany: Verlag, Palm & Enke, 1985.

BROWN-GUILLORY, ELIZABETH, ed. *Women of Color: Mother-Daughter Relationships in Twentieth-Century Literature*. Austin: University of Texas Press, 1996.

KELLEY, MARGOT. "A Minor Revolution: Chicano/a Composite Novels and the Limits of Genre." In *Ethnicity and the American Short Story*, edited by William E. Cain and Julia Brown. New York: Garland, 1997.

KURIBAYASHI, TOMOKO and JULIE THARP, eds. *Creating Safe Space: Violence and Women's Writing*. Albany: State University of New York Press, 1997.

MADSEN, DEBORAH L. *Understanding Contemporary Chicana Literature*. Columbia: University of South Carolina Press, 2000.

QUINTANA, ALVINA E., *Home Girls: Chicana Literary Voices*. Philadelphia: Temple University Press, 1996.

SALDÍVAR-HULL, SONIA. *Feminism on the Border: Chicana Gender Politics and Literature*. Berkeley: University of California Press, 2000.

REVIEW & RESOURCES

SparkNotes® Literature Guides